# STUDY GUIDE

for

# THE HOLY EUCHARIST

\*

Proposed Book of Common Prayer

\*

Ronald H. Miller

MOREHOUSE-BARLOW
Wilton, Connecticut

Text of The Holy Eucharist, Rites One and Two, A Penitential Order, Rites One and Two, and supplementary material (PROPOSED BOOK OF COMMON PRAYER pages 315-409) Copyright©1977 by Charles Mortimer Guilbert as Custodian of the Standard Book of Common Prayer. Reprinted by Permission.

Text of Study Guide Copyright
©1977 by Morehouse-Barlow Co., Inc.
78 Danbury Road
Wilton, Connecticut 06897

ISBN 0-8192-4075-3

Library of Congress Card No. 77-072492

*Printed in the United States of America*

# INTRODUCTION

As I started to write this study guide I received a presentation copy of the Standard Book of Common Prayer of 1892. It is a large, beautifully printed and illuminated volume which is a treasured addition to my library. A cursory examination of the "Order for the Administration of the Lord's Supper, or Holy Communion" in this 1892 book reveals major differences from what is found in the more familiar 1928 Book of Common Prayer. Indeed, over the years since the first Book of Common Prayer was published in 1549, change has been a regular note of Anglican worship, as it has been of Christian worship from the beginning. In every age Anglicans have tried to worship in forms which were faithful to the Gospel of God's love and redemption as revealed in Jesus Christ and which were shaped to be consistent with the Eucharist as it was celebrated in the earliest centuries of the Church's life. The development of the Eucharist, moreover, has balanced a common tradition which preserved continuity with the past and a continuous change which expressed that tradition in forms appropriate to the culture and patterns of thought of any particular age.

The Proposed Book of Common Prayer, page 13, states, "The Holy Eucharist, the principal act of Christian worship on the Lord's Day and other major Feasts, and Daily Morning and Evening Prayer, as set forth in this Book, are the regular services appointed for public worship in this Church." Although this might seem a new principle for those who know only the 1928 Book of Common Prayer, an examination of earlier Prayer Books would show that until 1892 the Eucharist was expected to be part of the normal Sunday service for Anglicans, as it has been for most Christians since the beginning of the Church. Even at times when celebrations of the Eucharist were infrequent there was rarely a denial of its centrality to worship. In the last several centuries there has been a growing recognition of the Eucharist as the appropriate service for Sundays.

This guide is written to help Episcopalians understand the revised forms for celebrating the Eucharist found in the Proposed Book of Common Prayer. The new elements of the services found here reflect a deepening understanding of the place of the Eucharist in the Church's life and in the lives of individual Christians. They also reflect a dramatic growth in knowledge of how the shape of the liturgy developed and changed. Only part of this knowledge can be touched upon in a study of this scope, but it is hoped the readers will be drawn to further and deeper study on their own.

For a long time, very little of this renewed sense of eucharistic worship has been allowed to filter down to the understanding of average lay people. The following example is perhaps extreme, but it is true. Some years ago, while preparing a group of young people for Confirmation, I asked what they thought happened during the service of Holy Communion. Their response, "We confess our sins, and then we receive the Body and Blood," revealed a rather impoverished, limited view of the sacrament. It is understandable that they should have received this impression when one remembers how the service used to be celebrated. One person, the celebrant, was busy doing something for the passive, immobile congregation. His activity could seem to be preparation for the two actions which the congregation actively performed: joining in the General Confession and going forward to receive the Sacrament. Their posture for most of the service, sitting or kneeling, reinforced this sense of passivity. No one would have taught the members of the Confirmation Class that the service was to be understood that way, but their own senses clearly told them so. By the end of our conference that class had been told that the Eucharist involved more than they said it did, but their own experience might well have had greater weight.

One of the discoveries of the Liturgical Movement, that group of people in various churches which in the last few decades has studied worship in history and has wrestled with what such history suggests for worship in our time, would help those young people grow in their understanding of the Eucharist. This is the recovery of the awareness that corporate worship involves the active, visible, and vocal participation of a number of people. Books of Common Prayer have been written on the assumption that a single minister would celebrate the entire service by himself. Rubrics, the directions for how services are to be conducted, in books as recent as the 1928 Prayer Book only recognize the corporate aspect by providing for the possibility of other ministers at the Eucharist reading the Epistle and Gospel, and by directing that a bishop, if present, might give the absolution and blessing.

In the Proposed Book there is a consistent principle that members of the assembled Church will perform many different functions in the service. The comments "Concerning the Celebration" on page 322 and 354 state how this is to be worked out at the Eucharist. Lay persons, deacons, priests, and bishops are to exercise their appropriate liturgical functions. Liturgy thus becomes truly the work of the people of God, not something done by a single active celebrant for a passive undifferentiated crowd or congregation. In the future, confirmation classes will have grown up seeing the Eucharist as something in which they may have an active part.

This recovery of active corporate participation is more important than it may seem at first. There has been a tendency to consider the sacrament in very individualistic terms and in many ways to divorce reception of communion from the celebration of the Eucharist. The preference for an early, spoken service so that music, sermon and other people would not intrude on the individual's devotions proceeds from such misconceptions, as does the occasional practice of leaving after the sermon or at some other point if a person does not want or feel ready to receive communion.

Any celebration of the Holy Eucharist involves more than just a sermon, confession, and communion. It is a *present* experience of the Gospel. To understand this, one must understand the Greek word *anamnesis*. There is no direct English equivalent; remembrance, memorial, recollection, representation, are all words which a dictionary might give as translations, but no one of them expresses all of the religious weight Christianity gives to the idea.

The Christian Gospel says that in the crucifixion and resurrection of Jesus, God revealed for all to see what his love means to the human race. Once and for all, that event, that dying and rising, changed the relationship between the Creator and those he had intended to represent him on earth. Eucharistic Prayer A, (PBCP page 362) summarizes this good news as well as anyone can, when it says, "Holy and gracious Father: In your infinite love you made us for yourself; and, when we had fallen into sin and become subject to evil and death, you, in your mercy, sent Jesus Christ, your only and eternal Son, to share our human nature, to live and die as one of us, to reconcile us to you, the God and Father of all." The question is how that event almost two thousand years ago becomes a real part of our contemporary experience. Somehow the time in between must be bridged. We cannot go back to that time, nor can that once-and-for-all event be repeated; however, the experience of Christians in every age has been that they become present at those saving events or those events become part of their lives. *Anamnesis* is the word used to label this experience of the transcendence of time.

The Greek word is composed of a prefix *ana*, "again," and a root, *mnesis*. The root is usually translated as "memory" or "remembering," but the idea is deeper than just that kind of mental exercise. It is closer to identity or self-recognition. Someone who has lost his memory has amnesia. An amnesiac does not know who he is, where he belongs, or how he got where he was found. An amnesiac has lost his identity or forgotten who he is. By our Baptism into Christ, by our share in the life of his body, we are given an identity, we are supplied with a past to help us know who we are. The Christian Eucharist is the occasion by which this identity is again made present. The individual and the community of which he is a member are brought to a recognition of this identity and given power to carry it into everyday life.

By our act of anamnesis the death and resurrection of our Lord become present. We praise God as we recall before him what he has done for us, and in that recollection he again restores us to our relationship with him. In the Eucharist this anamnesis is brought to our attention in the proclamation and exposition of Scripture, our record of God's self-revelation. It is acted out and directly experienced in the Great Thanksgiving and Communion. In Word and Sacrament, we are reminded of who we are, and we find the experience which makes that real in our lives. When the word "anamnesis" occurs later in this guide, it summarizes and recalls this discussion.

An adequate history of the Book of Common Prayer is beyond the scope of such a study guide. It will be helpful, however, for certain Prayer Books to be kept in mind during the following discussion. The eucharistic liturgy of the Church of England before the Reformation was the Latin Mass common throughout western Christendom. The first use of English at the Eucharist was an order for communion which was to be used during Mass after the priest's communion and which was published around 1548. This included several exhortations, a general confession and absolution, four sentences of scripture, and forms for the administration of communion. The first full service was published in 1549 in the first Book of Common Prayer. In many ways this book was like the various trial services the Episcopal Church has used between 1967 and 1976. The reactions to the 1549 book were mixed. It was criticized for going too far from the traditional services and for not going far enough. In general it can be described as a moderate effort to provide services in English, to reform medieval services into simpler forms which could be used more easily, and to correct some of the worst "abuses" of medieval devotion. The 1552 Prayer Book was a clear effort to make Anglican services more Protestant than even the 1549 book had been. After the brief reign of Mary Tudor, when England returned to the Roman Church, her sister Elizabeth I restored the 1552 book with only minor changes in 1559. This book was revised in 1662 at the restoration of the English monarchy. Although the text was little changed, the rubrics describing how the service was to be conducted went a long way toward replacing some of the reforming excesses of 1552.

During the seventeenth and eighteenth centuries a number of liturgies from the early Christian centuries were discovered and published. These transformed the understanding of the Eucharist held by Anglican theologians and provided impetus for the further revision of the Book of Common Prayer. The political system in England prevented such revision of the 1662 book, but various groups published (and perhaps used) services of the Eucharist which reflected this enriched understanding.

After the American Revolution, the American Anglicans had to establish their own national church independent of England, and this provided an opportunity to revise the Book of Common Prayer. The 1789 Book of Common Prayer was, in many ways, the first major revision since 1552. It reflected the influence of new liturgical scholarship mediated by the revisions of the Scottish Anglican bishops. In particular, the Eucharistic Prayer was restored to a shape more primitive than 1552 or the medieval missals. No one saw reason to change the language of the earlier books at that time. This book has been the standard for the American Church until the Proposed Book.

During the nineteenth century pressure again developed for change in the book. In 1892 and again in 1928 revisions were made which gave more freedom and flexibility in the celebration of the services, which restored some greater seasonal emphasis, and which reduced what was felt to be an excessive penitential tone. These revisions were conservative in that they did not add a great deal of different material to the services, but merely broadened the way in which material previously required at every celebration might be omitted. The 1892 book, for example, permitted the earlier Sunday pattern of full Morning Prayer, Litany, and Communion or Ante-Communion to be divided so that Sunday worship became either Morning Prayer, which was intended to be a daily office, or the Holy Communion. Aside from such increased flexibility, a shortening of the services and some moving around of certain parts, there had been almost no change in the text of the service since 1789 and little change of language since 1552.

During all this time there has been a revolution in our knowledge of the history and theology of worship, and there have been major changes in the way society and the world are perceived. The Latin missal reflected a certain conception of the relation between the Church and the world and between God and the Church. The Prayer Books in England and to a somewhat lesser degree here in America have sounded like the divinely established government at prayer. These cultural patterns no longer exist. The Proposed Book of Common Prayer is intended to reflect such change. We will see how some of these changes are expressed in the Holy Eucharist as this study proceeds. Other parts of the Prayer Book must wait for another guide.

Finally I must thank those who made it possible for me to write this guide. Although composed without reference to standard works of scholarship, many liturgical scholars will recognize some sources. Aside from my own copies of 1549, 1552, 1662, 1789, 1892, 1928, and the Proposed Book, I have used *Prayer Book Studies* IV, XVII, and 21 for certain information about sources. Shepherd's *Oxford American Prayer Book Commentary* provided confirming evidence at several points. It should be obvious, however, that the interpretation of evidence and any mistakes are only mine. The work is dedicated with thanks and affection to the Rector and people of St. Bartholomew's Church, Baltimore, Maryland.

# THE HOLY EUCHARIST: RITE ONE
## The Word of God

If for a moment we were to put ourselves in the position of starting fresh to write a service, the first question might be, "How should we begin?" The beginning of the service of Holy Communion in Books of Common Prayer has remained unchanged since 1552 when it was assumed that Morning Prayer and the Litany would always directly precede the service. Even though that has not been expected since the 1892 revision and, in fact, had ceased to be custom earlier in the nineteenth century, there has been no specific provision for the beginning of the service. A strict observance of the rubrics in the 1928 book would demand that the service begin immediately after the entrance of the minister or the opening hymn with either the Lord's Prayer or the prayer known as the Collect for Purity (1928 BCP, page 67). The custom in many places has been to preface the Collect for Purity with seasonal opening sentences from elsewhere in the book or with the salutation, "The Lord be with you" or simply, "Let us pray."

The intention behind such additions is what led to the opening acclamations in the Proposed Book. They praise God, in whose worship the congregation assembles, in a responsive form which calls that assembly together. The first of the choices, "Blessed be God . . ." is the customary opening of Eastern Orthodox services; the second, "Alleluia, Christ is risen," is the traditional Christian greeting during the Easter season; the third, "Bless the Lord who forgiveth all our sins," is reminiscent of passages in the Psalms and sets penitence in its proper perspective: we can praise God because he forgives our sins. All three provide a calling forth of the congregation to worship and a suitable ascription of glory to God consistent with the time or season.

The Collect for Purity is the last remnant from what was a longer service of preparation for the celebrant and his assistants, both lay and ordained. It expresses beautifully and succinctly the purpose of Christian worship and the realization that all true worship is the result of God's prior action. We have no secrets from God. To pretend with him is to deceive only ourselves. Only as purified by his Holy Spirit can we love God as we ought and give him the glory which is our purpose when we assemble for worship.

All Prayer Books since 1552 have directed that the Ten Commandments be recited after the Collect for Purity. This penitential exercise was seen as an extensive examination of conscience and a means by which the congregation could ask both God's forgiveness for breaking the Commandments and his grace to keep them in the future. The people's response: "Lord, have mercy upon us, and incline our hearts to keep this law" was the only form of the *Kyrie eleison* in Prayer Books until 1892, when its now familiar form was restored to be said when the Commandments were omitted. This was also the book which for the first time permitted the occasional omission of the Commandments with the understanding that they would be read at least once each Sunday.

The "Summary of the Law" was added to the Commandments in the 1789 American Book as a substitute or to be a more positive Christian alternative.

The Proposed Book recognizes that, for the most part, the Ten Commandments are no longer read regularly, and moves them out of the text of Rite One. It simply provides a rubric (on page 324) which indicates the point at which they might be read and where they can be found. The Proposed Book also permits the omission of the "Summary of the Law," and thus allows the Collect for Purity to be followed immediately by the *Kyrie*.

The function of the *Kyrie* has undergone a long process of change in the history of the Eucharist. It probably was introduced before the sixth century as part of a litany of intercession sung during the procession of the clergy to the sanctuary. *"Kyrie eleison"* is actually the only remaining fragment of Greek in non-Greek liturgies; its continued use thus becomes comparable to the Hebrew words, "Amen" and "Hallelujah" which everyone uses without surprise.

The exact translation of *Kyrie eleison* is "Lord, have mercy;" "upon us" only makes specific what is implied in the original phrase and extends the number of syllables in English to the same as the Greek. It is possible that this expansion was made to allow the retention of musical settings from before 1549 for use with that first Prayer Book. In 1552 the *Kyrie* was dropped in favor of the response to each Commandment.

It is not clear how the *Kyrie* was understood when it was first introduced into Christian liturgy, but one undocumented explanation of its use before then is that it was the cry of the crowds as the Roman emperor rode past. *"Kyrie eleison"* would mean "Sir, show pity" or, almost, "Lord, give a blessing," with the hope that he would toss a handful of coins. The word *eleison* comes from the same Greek word as "eleemosynary," referring to the giving of alms or the doing of good deeds. The popular understanding, "Forgive us" or "Have mercy on us miserable sinners" can only be traced back to the Middle Ages and the Latin *"Miserere nobis."* The *Kyrie* is actually a petition which comes from our trust in God because he has shown us his love in Christ. Because we have been shown this love we can cry, "Lord, show us your loving-kindness." The *Kyrie* is more a shout of triumph than a cry of supplication.

The new alternative, "Holy God, . . ." is introduced from Eastern Orthodox liturgies where it is used in much the same way as is *Kyrie eleison*. Musical settings of it are being published by various sources, and it should provide more variety in those seasons of the year when the *Gloria* is not sung.

The Proposed Book omits the collect which followed the Commandments, or the Summary of Law, or the *Kyrie,* and which asked God to help his people observe his Commandments. It has apparently been used less and less frequently.

As the final change in this opening section of the Eucharist, the *Gloria in excelsis* has been moved from the end of the service just before the blessing to this point following the *Kyrie*. In the 1549 Book of Common Prayer it was retained here in the beginning of the service where it had been in the pre-Reformation Latin mass. With the increase of penitential material in the 1552 book (such as the addition of the Ten Commandments) the *Gloria* was moved to the end of the service and has been retained there through the 1928 book.

The *Gloria* was originally used in the Daily Offices of the early Church; it was not so used in the early Books of Common Prayer, but it was restored to Evening Prayer in 1892. The *Gloria* was introduced into the Eucharist during the Middle Ages. It was originally used by the Bishop of Rome as his special prerogative at a Christmas Eve mass; subsequently other bishops wanted to use it not only at Christmas but on other festivals as well. Finally the privilege of its use was extended to all priests all of the time outside Advent and Lent.

The Rubrics give a fair amount of freedom to the beginning of the service. The 1928 sequence of Collect for Purity, Ten Commandments and/or Summary, and *Kyrie* may continue to be used, a different sequence, such as Opening Doxology and *Gloria,* might be used, or any combination of these elements. Not all of the possible parts should be used at the same service. The Additional Directions on page 406 suggest that the Great Litany could begin the service with the Litany's *Kyrie* leading directly to the Collect of the Day with its introductory salutation. Other parts of the Proposed Book provide additional ways in which the service might begin. See Holy Baptism or Confirmation for a simple expansion of the opening acclamations. The Order of Worship for the Evening is a very dramatic way to bring the congregation together at an evening celebration. The Proper Liturgies for Special Days give a number of appropriate ways to begin the service consistent with the season of the Church Year.

The use of these various options can go a long way to help set the tone of the service for a particular day. Easter Morning can be markedly different from the Third Sunday in Lent! This kind of freedom provides the enrichment the Proposed Book is designed to give, and it is a logical development from the flexibility which the 1892 and 1928 books allowed over earlier Prayer Books. Only a hundred years ago, the rubrics demanded that the Holy Communion begin with the Lord's Prayer (if Morning Prayer did not immediately precede the service), the Collect for Purity, the full Ten Commandments (there were no abbreviations of the longer Commandments), the Collect asking for help in keeping the Commandments, and the Collect of the Day; it was possible to add the Summary of the Law after the Commandments. The options and freedom of the Proposed Book give a welcome flexibility.

**The Collect of the Day**

In some sense, all that happens up to this point in the service is an extended preparation for the main attraction. In early centuries, the service apparently began with biblical readings which may have been introduced by a single prayer by the presiding minister. The series of Collects of the Day throughout the Church Year is the developed form of this practice. The study of the individual collects is an interesting subject in its own right; they come from various times and places in the life of the Church beginning with the fifth century when the earliest ones were first written down. Commentaries on the Proposed Book and the various *Prayer Book Studies* will provide some information about the sources.

The Collect of the Day is a major element in the service; it concludes the opening portion of the service, collects or brings together the prayers of the assembled congregation, leads into the lessons, and, frequently, sets the tone of the service in the context of the particular season of the Church year. In many parishes this solemnity is marked by singing the salutation and the Collect itself.

**The Lessons**

The first half of the Eucharist centers on the reading of the Bible, the Word of God. The preparatory part of the service leads up to the scripture readings; the sermon, creed, and intercessions relate the lessons to the daily lives of the congregation, allow its members to proclaim their response of faith, and give an initial expression of that response as the Gospel is related to the concerns expressed in the prayers.

Since the time of the seventh and eighth centuries when the traditional readings at the Eucharist began to be established, there has been a normal pattern of two: a reading from the New Testament Epistles, other New Testament writings, or, very occasionally, the Old Testament, and a reading from the Gospels. These readings were never totally static before the invention of printed books, and even since then, there have been slight modifications in the days for which readings were provided and in the exact readings themselves. Nevertheless, the Epistles and Gospels of the 1928 Prayer Book largely represent a tradition that goes back almost to the earliest surviving liturgical manuscripts, back to the times when these lists were established. For example, the Gospel for the First Sunday of Advent, Matthew 21:1-9, the Triumphal Entry of Jesus into Jerusalem before his Passion (commemorated as well in the Palm Sunday procession and blessing of palms, though that day's Gospel reading is from the story of Jesus's betrayal and crucifixion) goes back to manuscripts of the eighth and ninth centuries of books frequently ascribed to Pope Gregory the Great. Missals used on the continent of Europe during the Middle Ages had replaced it with a passage which looked forward to the Second Coming of Christ; but the medieval English missals had retained the older reading, and in the 1549 Book of Common Prayer the Cleansing of the Temple was added to the earlier reading. There are also readings, like those for the three Sundays before Lent, which have various local or temporal connections. These selections in books up to 1928 apparently date back to the barbarian invasions of Italy in the fifth and sixth centuries; such a reason does little to commend them to twentieth-century Americans.

In the various revisions of the Prayer Book, commemorations have been added or dropped (usually added), readings lengthened or shortened (usually lengthened), but the basic system was retained without change. One reason for the failure of any of the Books of Common Prayer to make substantial change was the assumption that everyone would attend Morning and Evening

Prayer every Sunday, and thus read Psalms and hear Old and New Testament readings. Until the 1892 revision it was assumed that Sunday morning service would include full Morning Prayer, the Litany and at least the "Ante-Communion" with sermon, and that the entire congregation would return for Evening Prayer, Baptism or the Catechism, and another sermon. The static and limited sets of readings at the Eucharist were extended and enriched by the lessons in the Daily Office. The Prayer Books of 1549 and 1552 assumed that people would hear almost all of the Old Testament once and the entire New Testament three times in the course of seven years through regular attendance at Sunday services. Later revisions appointed a specific set of Sunday readings because this system was not really satisfactory.

As did its immediate predecessors, *Services for Trial Use* and *Authorized Services 1973*, the Proposed Book appoints (on pages 888-931) a three-year cycle of three readings — Old Testament, Epistle and Gospel — as the principal set of readings for Sundays, holy days and other occasions. This is a revision of the three-year cycle originally established by the Roman Catholic Church after the Second Vatican Council. It has been adopted by a number of other Christian churches. The fact that most Western Christians will be using the same readings is an additional benefit to the great increase in the use of the Bible. It is true now, as it has not been since the earliest Books of Common Prayer, that readings at the Sunday service cover most of the Bible.

The reading of the Bible in liturgical worship is not intended to be a dry exercise in dull history nor a repetition of the incomprehensible. Season by season, Sunday by Sunday, the Church rehearses the acts of God which have called it into being, the process which created the community of his people assembled for worship. It is a formal, solemn act of anamnesis which helps the assembled community know how it came to be, why it does what it does, and what its mission is in the time and place it finds itself. Psalms, hymns, and anthems provide an immediate, active response to the readings.

**The Sermon**

The purpose of the sermon is to help individual members of the congregation to understand the readings in terms of their immediate situation and in the ways they normally think. Christ is present in the reading of the Gospel, but his presence is seen most clearly when the preacher points him out and calls the Church to respond to that presence. Without such interpretation and exposition there is danger that the reading of Scripture becomes a bare exercise in formalism.

**The Nicene Creed**

The readings from the Bible and the sermon are responded to and summarized in the recitation of the Nicene Creed. In Prayer Books up to 1928 the Creed preceded the sermon, but in other liturgies there was great variety in the Creed's position in the service and in the frequency of its recitation. The Proposed Book directs that it be said on Sundays and other major feasts.

Rite One of the Holy Eucharist contains two versions of the Nicene Creed. The first is the new translation made by the International Consultation on English Texts, and the second is the version contained in Books of Common Prayer since 1549.

The Creed commonly called "Nicene" is actually the product of the first two Ecumenical Councils. The first, held at Nicaea in 325 A.D., produced a creed which condemned and denied the Arian heresy. In 381 the Council at Constantinople revised and expanded this creed into the form which has come down to us. The ICET version is a direct translation from the original Greek text as adopted at the Council; thus it is a creed which expresses the faith of the Church, what *we* believe as members of the Church. At Baptism and at Confirmation, each individual makes a personal confession of faith in God. At the Eucharist we are reminded of our common faith, and we join ourselves to the company of people who believe in God the Father, God the Son, and God the Holy Spirit. There are a number of changes in the new translation; all of them reflect the fact that this is a fresh modern translation from the original Greek.

The traditional version, which is printed in response to substantial demand that it be retained, was translated into sixteenth-century English from the Latin version. The differences between the two versions reflect the problems encountered when translations of a text are made in different periods. The original has not changed in meaning, but because of intermediate versions and the time-bound character of language, the same concepts must be expressed in different words. The book does not actually contain two creeds, but the same basic text as expressed in the language of two different eras.

Theological and historical commentaries on the creed can be found in many books, and our only purpose here is to understand its place in the liturgy. Although its liturgical recitation was a celebration of the theological orthodoxy of those who began reciting it, it can best be seen now as a summary proclamation of the God we worship as he has revealed himself in scripture and in history, as well as in the lives of Christians.

## The Prayers of the People

The faithful response to God's call in scripture, as reflected upon in the sermon and summarized in the creed, has its logical completion in the act of sharing with those who do not know him the good news of God's loving concern. The first expression of this is the Prayer of Intercession.

Some of the earliest accounts of the Christian Eucharist speak extensively of prayer by the assembled Christian community for the Church and the world around it. This has been a part of the Eucharist ever since. The shape and content have varied widely as the Church found itself in different situations, but the principle has been consistently maintained. Eastern Orthodox liturgies have retained what is most likely the most ancient style of prayer, the litany, in which an object of intercession is introduced by the leader, to which the congregation adds a familiar, repeated response, *Kyrie eleison*, "Hear us, good Lord," or some such phrase. In the Latin Mass these prayers were dropped in favor of additions to the Prayer of Consecration. The 1549 BCP retained the Mass's structure of intercession within the Consecration by including a long prayer for the whole state of Christ's Church after the offertory and the Preface and Sanctus. In 1552 this prayer was moved to immediately after a collection of alms for the poor and was revised into roughly the form it has retained through the 1928 revision. The only major changes since 1552 have been the restoration of a commemoration of those who have died and, in the American books, the substitution of other political leaders for the king.

The form for this prayer in Rite One, page 328ff, retains almost all of the traditional wording. The following are the only exceptions: since the offertory has not yet taken place, there is no reference to alms and oblations; the petition for civil government has been rewritten in light of the need to pray for all in authority around the world, not just Christian rulers and magistrates; there is a new petition which asks that all people may be faithful stewards of creation; and there is provision in a number of appropriate places for the inclusion of the names of specific people who need the Church's prayers, the sick, the dead, those in ministry or government.

One source of dissatisfaction with this prayer in the recent past has been that it was an extremely long monologue at a place where, for much of Christian history, people have been able to add their voices to the Church's prayers. The Proposed Book gives two ways the concern may be met: any form of prayer which fulfills the directions on page 383 may be substituted for the prayer printed here, or the congregation may make a response after each paragraph of the traditional prayer. Either of these possibilities restores to the people a vocal part in what are, after all, their own prayers.

**The Confession of Sin**

As Christians approach the Lord's table they sense both the greatness of God's gift of salvation and the failure in their lives to reflect that gift. In one form or another from about the fourth century reception of Holy Communion has been tied to some formal acknowledgement of the communicant's sinfulness. The form has ranged from a substantial penitential retreat, to private confession and absolution, to some general act of confession and absolution. The succession of Prayer Books has continued this tradition. As we move from the 1928 book back through its predecessors, we discover that penitential parts of services which in 1928 were only required on a limited number of occasions and which have frequently been omitted entirely, had been required more and more frequently in the past. As we have seen already, the Ten Commandments have fallen into disuse where once they were required at every celebration. Similarly, the long exhortations, which in 1928 were printed at the end of the Holy Communion, had been printed previously in the body of the service with rubrics directing their regular use. In particular, the first one in the 1928 book, which recalls the great benefits of the sacrament and the danger of receiving it lightly or in a state of sinfulness, had been required at every celebration from 1552 on. It was required in the 1892 book at least once each Sunday; only in 1928 was the requirement changed to three times a year.

Although these long, somber homilies on sin and repentance have been removed from any regular use, the Proposed Book retains the regular Invitation to Confession, the traditional Confession and Absolution, and the scriptural passages identified as the "Comfortable Words." There have been a few other minor changes. The introductory rubric recognizes that a confession may have been made at the beginning of the service (see A Penitential Order, Rite One, PBCP pages 319f), and that there may be occasions on which it is appropriate to omit confession and absolution. Such omissions, however, are clearly to be exceptions.

The Invitation, "Ye who do truly and earnestly repent . . ." has had one change in the new book, which reflects a long-standing shift of custom. No longer is it expected that only some members of the congregation would "take this holy sacrament to [their] comfort"; this phrase is omitted, and the invitation to "draw near with faith" means not to move forward to the chancel, as it did through the eighteenth century, but to make a spiritual approach. With the general relaxing of habits of posture at services, even the bidding "devoutly kneeling" may cease to be redundant. There is provided an alternate to this invitation which simply bids the congregation to join in the confession.

The traditional form of the General Confession is included as the first form in Rite One; however, many people have felt that the particular rhetoric in which it is written is too elaborate to speak truly of our modern sense of sin. The alternate confession, which is common to all major public services in the Proposed Book, expresses repentance and petition for forgiveness — significantly, for "what we have left undone" as well as for our misdeeds — not in the extreme language of the sixteenth-century form, but in simpler, more contemporary patterns of thought. This new form actually looks back to the "Summary of the Law" as the pattern for Christian life.

The other changes in this section are relatively minor modifications in the "Comfortable Words." This traditional introduction to these biblical readings no longer uses that misleading announcement from earlier Prayer Books. They were intended to be comfortable in the older sense of strengthening, and most biblical scholars have serious questions about the ascriptions. However, the traditional readings in traditional language are retained, with only a single alteration and an illuminating expansion of the last saying. It is now possible to omit them entirely or to select one or more from the four passages which had been required.

**The Peace**

"The Proclamation of the Word of God" concludes with the greeting and response, "The peace of the Lord be always with you." "And with thy spirit." Perhaps no single thing has been so upsetting to some people during the recent period of trial use. Many other people have found it the most positive of the changes. Something which causes such strong feelings cannot be taken lightly.

From the earliest accounts of the Church's worship, as indeed from the New Testament itself, we find that Christians have considered themselves to be members (arms, legs, feet, hands) of the body of Christ. This kind of unity is the context in which we assemble for worship, in which we learn about God's love for us and for all humanity, and in which we experience our own redemption. It is fitting, therefore, that this community assembled for worship express the basis of its unity and the love which draws it together. Even if there is no ceremonial physical expression during the service, at least the verbal exchange of the Peace between the celebrant and congregation expresses the sense of unity at the center of the service. The Proposed Book suggests that members of the congregation and the ministers might greet each other, but it does not require this nor direct how it might be done. Some of the strongest sayings of Jesus condemn worship which is offered in the context of hatred or anger. By greeting those around us in love, there can be a sign that we approach God's presence at peace with one another.

The Peace has been placed at different parts of the liturgy in various times and places. At its present location, it gives a summary of what has gone before, it concludes the prayers of intercession and penitence, and it shows the readiness of the congregation for what follows. In the Roman Mass it had been placed after the Lord's Prayer and before the Communion (the Additional Directions of the Proposed Book, page 407, permit its use at this point). This placement may well be derived from the distinctly Roman custom of the *fermentum:* a fragment of bread from the bishop's Eucharist was brought to the local celebration and at this point mixed with the elements of the local celebration to unite the latter to the former. In any case, although something can be said for approaching the Lord's table in his peace, a stronger case can be made for offering our gifts for that table in the unity of his peace. When there is to be no Communion, the service concludes at this point with the Lord's Prayer and the Peace, followed by the Grace or a blessing.

## The Celebration of the Holy Communion

Whereas the first half of the Eucharist centers around the reading of the Bible, with the proclamation of the Gospel as its high point, the second half celebrates in word and deed the same mighty acts of God described in the scriptures. The Liturgy of the Word can be traced back to synagogue services like those Jesus is recorded in the Gospels to have attended. The liturgy of the Holy Communion goes back to religious or ritual meals common in Judaism from before the time of Jesus. Much of Christian tradition and the devotional practices it inspired has focused almost exclusively on the last meal Jesus shared with his disciples before his death and on what he said at that time. One of the discoveries of recent liturgical scholarship has been that the absolute centrality of this meal can be enriched if it is seen in the context of Jewish ritual meals, of the kind of prayers common to these meals, and of all the other meals Jesus is recorded to have shared with his followers before and after his death and resurrection. A token of the shift in understanding can be seen in the fact that from the 1662 BCP through the 1967 Liturgy of the Lord's Supper the central prayer of the Eucharist was called the Prayer of Consecration. Since 1970, when *Prayer Book Studies* 21: *The Holy Eucharist*, which lies behind the Proposed Book and its predecessors, was published, this central prayer has been called the Great Thanksgiving. This shift is not in any sense intended to deny the role of the prayer in terms of Christ's presence in the elements; rather, it is a shift in emphasis or perspective which sees the principal concern being the praise and thanksgiving to God for what he has done, through which the congregation shares again in the life of Christ present in its midst. Of particular importance has been the discovery that the prayers Jesus and his earliest followers used (some of which are found in the earliest post-biblical accounts of the Christian Eucharist) praised and blessed God for creation, for the life of his people, and for the way in which he had redeemed them and established them as a nation. The largest part of the prayers would be addressed to God in terms of blessing, or praise, or thanksgiving. They would conclude with petitions that he would finally establish his kingdom, and intercessions for the people, the nation, and those in need. In other words, the worshipping community recalled to God and to themselves his greatness and love as it had been known in the past, praised and thanked him for these benefits, and asked that their effects might be found in the lives of the praying community. The recalling in praise of the history of salvation made those praying present at the events which had worked their salvation and made the effects of those past acts present in their daily lives. Such prayers are clearly related to the major prayer of the Eucharist. As the history of its development has been uncovered, it has become more and more clear that the Eucharist itself is this kind of recalling before God and the assembly of the works of redemption with prayers that the fruits of redemption may be known in the lives of those present. The offering and consecration of the bread and wine become not the end purpose of the celebration, but the occasion around which the proclamation of praise and thanksgiving is centered. Thus there is the shift from "Prayer of Consecration" to "Great Thanksgiving."

Another complex issue behind the form of the Eucharist in the Proposed Book is the question of "the shape of the liturgy," as Dom Gregory Dix's classic of liturgical history is titled. All of the accounts of the Last Supper recall that at the beginning of a meal Jesus took bread, blessed it (we might call it, "said grace"), and broke it so that he might distribute pieces to those present at the meal. This action was the normal way to begin a Jewish meal; it became important on that occasion only because of the interpretation he gave as he distributed the broken fragments of bread to the company. Similarly, all accounts say that after supper he took a cup, gave thanks over it, and shared it among those present. This was the high point of any Jewish meal. A prayer of thanksgiving was said over this final cup which blessed God for what he had done and for the meal just concluded. Jesus's action was again remarkable here because of the interpretation he gave as he passed the wine around.

The Great Thanksgiving, like the Prayers of Consecration before it, developed from this thanksgiving over the cup and from other similar prayers, as was mentioned above. The surprising thing is the way these two separate sets of actions — one, taking bread, giving thanks, breaking it and sharing it, and two, taking wine, giving thanks over it and sharing it — came to be combined in the classic pattern of the Eucharist known from accounts which date back to the second century. The meal was dropped out, and the sequence became: taking bread and wine, giving thanks over them with a recalling of Jesus' commands at that final supper, breaking the bread and sharing the bread and wine among the people present.

For most of Christian history this shape has remained constant. The great prayer of thanksgiving and consecration was preceded by the taking of bread and wine, usually while Psalms were being sung. After the solemn proclamation of the Eucharistic Prayer and the Lord's Prayer, the consecrated bread would be broken for distribution, and the clergy and members of the congregation would receive their Communion, have a short prayer after Communion, and depart with a ceremonial dismissal or blessing. As time passed this simple outline became overlaid and almost hidden with additional ceremonies, additional prayers, and other devotional practices. There were two particular changes which had important influences on the development of the Prayer Books: it became more and more rare for lay people to receive Communion at the Eucharist (they would make their annual Communion immediately after their Easter confession); and the Eucharistic Prayer — indeed, the entire service — came to be understood more as an offering to God in intercession for the living and the dead or for some other specific request, than as a prayer of praise and thanksgiving which might contain some intercessions. The heavy emphasis on penitence in the Prayer Book Communion service came from an effort to prepare the congregation for Communion at each weekly celebration and to encourage them to make their Communion frequently. The medieval emphasis on the offering of the Eucharist with the conviction that as a result God would do what he was asked finally led to the buying and selling of Masses for just about any imaginable goal and to the popular conception of God as the terrible judge who could only be bribed into forgiving his people. This, of course, was the scandal which led to the Reformation. For our present purposes, this is important as the source of Anglican resistance to any language or to any ceremonial action in the Eucharistic Prayer which suggested offering or prayers for the dead.

With this general background to the Eucharist in mind, we can turn to the Holy Communion as it was found in the Prayer Books which lie behind the Proposed Book. The easiest and most accurate description of the eucharistic action in the 1549 book is to say that the Prayer of Consecration represented a simplification and recomposition into English idiom of most of the Roman Canon of the Mass. The words and the theological imagery are not the same, but the shape and apparent intention are fairly close. The one new note was the addition of an order for Communion of the congregation, with Confession and Absolution, Comfortable Words and Prayer of Humble Access after the Consecration, Lord's Prayer, and Peace.

With the 1552 book there was a radical effort to work out a service which was far removed from the "medieval superstitions" only partially corrected in 1549. Portions of prayers were dropped and the sequence was radically rearranged so that hardly any idea of offering or consecration could be found.

The details of this change can be discovered by an examination of the 1549 and 1552 books. The subsequent history in 1662, 1789, 1892, and 1928 was the gradual restoration of what was, in fact, a sequence of action and prayer older than the abuses attacked at the Reformation. Of particular importance was the adoption in the 1789 book of a Prayer of Consecration which had the shape of eucharistic prayers in the early Church. In 1928 the full ancient sequence was restored, except that the offertory was still displaced before the prayer for the whole state of Christ's Church and the penitential order, and the Peace, the *Benedictus* after the *Sanctus*, and a separate Fraction were again absent. The Proposed Book adopts the ancient sequence of prayers, peace and offertory, and restores these other traditional elements.

Rite One includes all of the elements of the 1549 book in largely the same language, with some additional alternatives and greater flexibility. The most important shift in the new book is to move the intercessions and confession back before the Offertory. This sequence corresponded to the pattern of the early Church and has become standard for modern liturgical revision. Elements such as the Peace, the *Benedictus* after the *Sanctus*, the *Agnus Dei* and the several paragraphs after the institution narrative had been rejected on the erroneous belief that they were late medieval corruptions. While the Prayer of Consecration was restored to its earlier state in 1789, these other elements are now present in the Prayer Book for the first time since 1549. Their recovery has been based on the discoveries of liturgical history which showed that they were part of the Eucharist from earliest times.

Page 333 is the beginning of the eucharistic action proper. This division is marked by the title at the top of the page, and only several brief rubrics stand between the title and the central action, the offering and proclamation of the Great Thanksgiving. Since the selection of one or more offertory sentences is at the discretion of the celebrant, the text of the service is not cluttered with the entire set of choices as earlier Prayer Books were. The rubric simply directs the celebrant to the appropriate pages. This is one example of the way the Proposed Book has made it easier to follow the service. Variable materials and materials used only occasionally are not printed in the body of the service: the Ten Commandments, Proper Prefaces, and the long Exhortation are other examples.

The simple action of Jesus in taking bread and wine has become elaborate over the centuries. It is still intended to be just the first step in the eucharistic action, and therefore should not overshadow what follows. Provision is made for members of the congregation to bring the offering of bread and wine, with money or other gifts, to the minister who prepares the altar, but this does not demand any elaborate marching up and down. Overly elaborate music, patriotic hymns, and fussy elevations and presentations can make the Great Thanksgiving, on which attention should be centered, anti-climactic.

## The Great Thanksgiving

Eucharistic Prayer I, which is printed in the body of the service, has been retained without change from the 1928 book. 1928 was the first book to restore the primitive order to this prayer; earlier books, since 1552, had interposed the Prayer of Humble Access between the Preface/*Sanctus* sequence and the beginning of the Prayer of Consecration and thereby destroyed any sense that the Preface was the beginning of the Prayer of Consecration. The Proposed Book permits the addition of the *Benedictus Qui Venit;* it had actually been used for some time by parts of the Church.

The continued presence of this Great Thanksgiving here in the body of the service is witness to the strong feelings of many Church members. Among liturgical scholars it has not been in great favor. The critics argue that the theology expressed in the prayer is limited, almost impoverished: the praise of God does not include many things for which he should be praised, the Christology ignores Christ's role in creation and his Incarnation, and it barely mentions such things as his resurrection, ascension, or second coming. Those who support its continued use express devotion to it on the basis of its familiarity, its "beauty of expression," and its "traditional" theology. The compromise of printing this prayer in the text and providing a satisfactory alternate form beginning on page 340 is a classic Anglican solution.

The opening dialogue, called the *Sursum Corda,* and the Preface or first part of the prayer are organized around the idea of giving thanks and praise to God the Father, in union with those who worship him in heaven, by singing the *Sanctus.* On Sundays and other occasions specific reasons for this praise and thanksgiving are included by the use of a preface appropriate to the day, the season, or the specific occasion of the service. These are found on pages 344-349 and will be examined later.

After the *Sanctus,* the prayer continues the praise of the Father for his goodness in sending the Son to die for our redemption. In quite technical, almost legal language the prayer remembers that his death once and for all made satisfaction for the sins of the whole world, and that he established a memorial of that death to be continued until he comes again. The occasion on which Jesus instituted this memorial forms the next part of the prayer; the

Last Supper is recalled in word and deed. The breaking of the bread, which was done at this point from 1662 to 1928, has been postponed, and the directions for manual actions of the celebrant have been simplified. In obedience to his institution the assembled church celebrates and makes the commanded memorial (anamnesis) by offering God's gifts of bread and wine while remembering Christ's death and resurrection and heartily thanking God for the benefits they brought. The Father is asked to bless these gifts in union with his Word (or Son) and the Holy Spirit so that in obedience to Christ's command and in remembrance of his death the congregation may partake of his Body and Blood. God is asked to accept this sacrifice of praise and thanksgiving and, on the basis of Christ's merits and death, to grant to the whole Church forgiveness of sins and all other benefits of his suffering. The members of the congregation offer their lives in sacrifice to God with the request that all who share in the Communion may receive Christ's Body and Blood, be filled with God's blessing, and be united with Christ. Although their sins make the congregation unworthy to offer any sacrifice, God is asked to accept this obligatory memorial through Christ with whom, as they are united by the Holy Spirit, the Church offers all honor and glory to the Father. The Amen signifies that all people present assent in this prayer.

Once this has been done, the prayer Christ taught can be prayed with confidence to "Our Father, who art in heaven." In the history of the Eucharist, the Lord's Prayer has at various times been placed before or after the people's Communion. 1928 was the first Prayer Book since 1549 to restore it here before Communion where it has most often been seen as a summary of the Eucharistic Prayer and a preparation for the reception of the Sacrament. "Give us this day our daily bread" is sometimes interpreted to mean the eucharistic bread of life.

**The Breaking of the Bread**

This final section of the service includes not only the Fraction (as the breaking is called) in imitation of Jesus' action at the Last Supper, but also a series of optional Communion devotions, the distribution of the Sacrament, and the conclusion of the service with a postcommunion prayer, blessing of the people, and an optional dismissal. As was mentioned above, (page 21), the breaking of the bread originally had a practical purpose: it was how the large loaves were shared among those present at a meal. In the early centuries of the Christian Eucharist the Fraction still was functional since it was custom to use loaves of regular bread. In the Western Church from about the tenth century, there developed the use of wafer breads; however, at the time of the Reformation the English Church returned to the use of leavened bread, and it was only in the latter part of the nineteenth century that wafers again began to be used. There is a move on the part of a number of parishes to return to everyday bread in such a way as to make apparent the share all Christians have in the single loaf. Even if the customary wafers are used, a fraction has become traditional, and it reminds those present both of the breaking of Christ's Body on the cross and of many individuals sharing in the one Communion.

The occasion of breaking the bread became a center around which various devotional practices developed. The anthem on page 337 was a fraction sentence in 1549. The *Agnus Dei* ("Lamb of God") was a traditional communion anthem in the Roman Mass retained only in 1549. It has been used in many parishes, although not printed in the Prayer Book until now.

The Prayer of Humble Access is made optional and has one change from its traditional Anglican form. The clauses "that our sinful bodies may be made clean by his body and our souls washed through his most precious blood" have been omitted. These indicated a distinction which has always been more imagined than real. The effect of Christ's presence in the sacramental elements is indivisible, and the omitted phrases were probably intended to be simple rhetorical flourishes, but they have become misleading. Their omission is not likely to be missed, since the remaining parts of the prayer flow smoothly.

The optional invitation on page 338 serves to tell the congregation to approach to altar. It has been traditional to insert either a spoken invitation or a gesture at the point people should begin to leave their pews. In addition to the traditional sentences of administration, two other choices are provided; both of them are short enough to be said to each communicant. It should be noted that everything except the act of the Fraction and the reception of the elements with some sentence is optional. This gives the freedom to select elements appropriate to the day or season. One would not expect to hear everything read at a single service.

There has been much discussion about what should be done when insufficient elements have been consecrated. Rather than requiring the repetition of the bulk of the Eucharistic Prayer, as has been customary since 1789, the Proposed Book provides a short form on page 408 which briefly summarizes the basic elements of the Eucharistic Prayer.

The postcommunion prayer is retained with some minor changes and with permission for the congregation to say it with the celebrant. In traditional language it expresses the effects of participation in the sacrament and a request that God's grace will produce those effects in the lives of these communicants. The few omissions lighten the style a little but do not change anything of substance.

The service concludes with the traditional blessing, "The peace of God . . ." and an optional dismissal. A shorter blessing which removes the repetition of the Peace is provided as an alternate form. The dismissals emphasize that the worship of God just concluded is both a cause for thanksgiving and an impetus for mission in the world.

## Other materials in Rite One

### Eucharistic Prayer II

The intention of this alternative form of the Great Thanksgiving is to preserve the style and most of the content of the 1928 Eucharistic Prayer while correcting the main criticisms noted above (page 24). Thus, God is glorified for creation, for the creation of mankind in his image, and for the Incarnation of his Son. The heavy, repetitious, legal language of the paragraph after the *Sanctus* has been simplified, as has the Reformation argument which insists over and over again on the oneness and completeness of Christ's sacrifice. The extremely heavy emphasis and frequent mention of the congregation's sinfulness and repentance after the institution narrative has been moderated somewhat. There is a clear reference to the expectation of Christ's coming again, and the petition that God would bless the gifts speaks somewhat more objectively about Christ's presence in the elements. The final paragraph expresses in a somewhat less heavy fashion the prayer for the fruits of Communion in the whole Church, not just the present congregation. This prayer deserves frequent use in Rite One celebrations.

### Offertory Sentences

Both the 1892 and 1928 books made changes in the biblical passages to be read at the time of the collection. Most of those added in 1928 do not seem to have been widely used. The selection on pages 343 and 344 of the Proposed Book speaks more directly of offering to God something of what he has given and drops the earlier emphasis on doing good works for those in need.

## Proper Prefaces

The use of variable prefaces which change with the seasons of the Church Year is unique to Western liturgies. At some times in the past there have been prefaces for almost every day. In the 1549 book the number was reduced to five: Christmas, Easter, Ascension, Whitsunday or Pentecost, and Trinity Sunday. Since 1552 these have been said through the Octave, that is, the full week following the feast. In the 1928 book prefaces were added for the Octaves of Epiphany and All Saints Day and one for use on the days of the Purification, Annunciation and Transfiguration. This still meant that only seven weeks of the year had a proper preface.

In the Proposed Book, prefaces are provided for all Sundays and seasons of the Church Year. Rather than simply giving dignity to a few major festivals, proper prefaces now give a distinctive seasonal note to most celebrations. In the same way that the collect of the day sets the tone for the Liturgy of the Word, the proper prefaces bring to the center of the Eucharist a specific aspect of the mighty acts by which redemption was accomplished. The work of Christ is spread across time in a way which allows the assembled Christians to live through these salvific events, as it were, to become present to them as they are rehearsed in the Liturgy.

## A Penitential Order: Rite One

Finally we will examine the penitential materials which are placed before Rite One, pages 316-321. From 1552 through the life of the 1892 book, at least once a Sunday, there would be read to the congregation a lengthy address on the importance of receiving Communion and the danger in receiving it without a proper understanding and appreciation of God's grace and love in providing these holy Mysteries. These exhortations (1928 BCP pages 85-89) are examples of the best and the worst of English Reformation piety. Although written with good style, they are heavy and ponderous as they exalt the righteousness and majesty of God and demean our weak and sinful nature. The decline in their use in recent times is understandable, for they were defeating their own stated intention — to get people to Communion more frequently.

The Exhortation on page 316 is a fresh composition inspired by the earlier ones; much of its content is drawn from them, as well. Here, however, as in Eucharistic Prayer II, God's love is praised for more than just our redemption, the effect of the Sacrament is more than just the forgiveness of sins, and the tone is less thundering and threatening. All in all, it is an excellent piece of work and deserves to be used sparingly but regularly with all congregations.

The Ten Commandments begin on page 317. Their use is no longer required at the Eucharist, although there is permission to use them after the Collect for Purity in Rite One. They are drawn from Exodus 20:1-17. With the exception of the restoration of the full first verse, they are printed only in the short form which was permitted for the first time in the 1928 book.

One of the practices used experimentally during the period of Trial Use was to begin the Liturgy with Confession and Absolution which would then be omitted later in the service. This practice met with some favor; the presence of the Penitential Order reflects this opinion. After an opening greeting, the Ten Commandments may be read. Then follows one or another of several New Testament passages, the General Confession and Absolution. If the Eucharist is to follow, this leads directly to the hymns before the Collect of the Day. If it is to be used as a separate office, for example, on the night before the Eucharist, in a conference setting, additional prayers and the Grace or blessing would conclude the Order.

# THE HOLY EUCHARIST: RITE TWO

A great deal of the discussion of Rite One is equally applicable to Rite Two. The structure and the constituent parts are common to both rites. Our discussion of Rite Two will deal with the general questions of ICET versions and the use of contemporary English for worship, and then discuss those texts of Rite Two which are different from Rite One.

The act of worship appeals to or works through many facets of the human personality: our aesthetic sense, our perception of symbols, the images in which we perceive the world, and even our inclinations of bodily posture. All of these and more contribute to our experience of God in our worship. This means that only part of the effect of worship is mediated through the words of the service. One of the reactions against the 1967 Liturgy of the Lord's Supper came from people who did not want or did not understand ceremonial changes such as standing for some of the prayers in the Eucharist. Their reaction against this had no direct bearing on the text of the rite, but rather they were making clear that things other than the words used had an impact on their experience. The same impact, in a positive way, can be seen in the approval given changes of building or music which encourage a greater reverence in the service. Words are not all of worship; they are, however, extremely important because they interpret and give specific meaning to the non-verbal aspects of worship. The character of the language, therefore, is extremely important.

When the Standing Liturgical Commission analyzed the responses to the 1967 trial service, they discovered two distinctly opposed reactions to the language of that service. There was a large number of respondents who did not want any change in the language of the liturgy; they wanted to continue to worship in the same traditional "Prayer Book" language. There was an equally large number who wanted to worship in contemporary language, in language related to everyday speech. The Rite Two services are intended to provide for the latter, as Rite One services do for the former.

The two styles differ in more ways than just in the use of certain pronouns and verb forms. Tudor English, the English in which the 1549, 1552, and 1559 Prayer Books were written, is the language found in documents from the reigns of Henry VIII and his children, Edward VI, Mary, and Elizabeth I. It stood much closer to the sources of the English language than does our formal speech today. The French which had been spoken by the upper classes after the Norman conquest in 1066, the Latin which was used in Church and university, and the Anglo-Saxon which was, in its various dialects, the language of the common people, had all contributed to the characteristics of the formal language of the time, the language into which traditional Latin liturgies were translated for the 1549 and 1552 Prayer Books.

The flowing together of Anglo-Saxon and French produced one element of "Prayer Book" style, that is, the tendency to express a single idea by the use of two words, one from German by way of Anglo-Saxon and one from Latin through French. "Bless and sanctify," "prayers and supplications," "comfort and succor," and "love and charity" are just a few examples quickly gleaned from the Rite One Eucharist. This was probably a necessary technique to communicate in the fourteenth and fifteenth centuries, when English was emerging as a single language, and it was probably a reasonable element of style in the sixteenth century. It is not characteristic of contemporary English.

The debt to Latin was first for theological language. Western theology had been written in Latin since the second and third centuries, and it was the language for worship from at least the fourth century. The main debt to Latin, however, was one of style. Latin makes heavy use of various kinds of dependent clauses as a way to organize and articulate ideas. This tendency was carried over into the sixteenth-century Prayer Book translations of liturgical texts where it was reinforced by the formal rhetorical style of the royal and judicial courts. (Thomas Cranmer was the guiding force behind the early Prayer Books, and his specialty was Canon Law.) An examination of Eucharistic Prayer I, for example, will show that it is composed of only a few long, elaborate sentences. These sentences express the relative importance of their ideas by the independence or the dependence and subordination of the clauses in which the ideas are stated. To many modern ears, such long, complicated structures serve more to confuse and distract than to enlighten.

The language of Rite Two services, on the other hand, reflects the way in which English has evolved over the last four hundred years. The impetus behind the use of parallel French and Saxon words has disappeared, even as the vocabulary has continued to be enriched. There has been a simplification of style which replaced the long, complicated sentences with simpler forms which derive their impact from a greater immediacy and a more vivid pattern of expression.

Critics of the modern-language services have made very harsh comments about the contemporary language of those services. Some of their mildest accusations have been that it is banal and flat. These critics are entitled to their opinions, but their comments on language need to be seen in the context of their overall attitude toward liturgical renewal. Generally speaking, they reject any possibility of substantial change in the 1928 book. No one has suggested that 1892, 1662, 1552, or the old Latin missal be restored, let alone that worship be conducted according to the ancient forms in Greek or Hebrew. Change up to 1928 was good, but any substantial change since then is not. People who feel this way would not accept the use of contemporary English.

There are also many people whose devotional lives have developed with the traditional rites, and for them the switch to contemporary English requires a substantial adjustment. The transition does not come easily, but many people have found that once time is allowed for it to become familiar, contemporary language works well for worship and private prayer.

There is little more that can be said to defend the language of Rite Two services. Reverence, dignity, beauty, and clarity are the marks of these modern services. The future of Anglican worship will probably be traced back to the modern language portions of the Proposed Book as earlier books have looked back to 1552 and 1549.

Rite Two uses new translations of those texts in the service which are common to all Christian Churches. These were prepared by a commission of scholars from the Churches in English speaking countries. The ICET (International Consultation on English Texts) versions of the *Gloria, Kyrie,* Nicene Creed, *Sursum Corda, Sanctus* and *Benedictus,* Lord's Prayer, and *Agnus Dei* were first used in *Services for Trial Use* and appear in the Proposed Book in their final, revised form. Aside from their merit as fresh, contemporary translations based on the original texts (not on late Latin versions as were those traditionally used in Books of Common Prayer) these prayers we have in common will come to be used by all English-speaking Christians. No longer, for example, will we wonder in ecumenical prayer whether to say "debts" or "trespasses" in the Lord's Prayer. The specifics of some of these translations will be discussed at their place in the service. It should be observed, however, that when they differ from the traditional forms it is because of more accurate translation or in the interest of clear contemporary English.

## The Proclamation of the Word of God

The Holy Eucharist, Rite Two begins on page 355; it is preceded on pages 350-353 by a contemporary translation of the Ten Commandments and by a Penitential Order: Rite Two. (The Exhortation, page 316, can also be used with this order since its language is not particularly archaic.) The use of these optional materials was discussed on pages 28f.

Rite Two itself begins with the Proclamation of the Word of God. The opening acclamations and the Collect for Purity illustrate the minor changes which are sometimes enough to effect a shift from traditional to contemporary language or vice versa; minor changes of verb forms or pronouns suffice if the element being changed is not especially time-bound. There are other occasions when a traditional text is not so easily changed. The Prayer for All Sorts and Conditions of Men, which in American books was found in Morning and Evening Prayer and in the Proposed Book is on page 814, was added to the 1662 book among the Occasional Prayers; it is an example of a prayer in which both the language and the patterns of thought are so time-bound that a few changes could not make it a contemporary prayer in the way the simple changes of Rite Two do.

The *Gloria*, or other hymn of praise (for example the *Te Deum*, page 95 or *Pascha nostrum*, page 83), is to be sung or said from Christmas through the feast of the Epiphany, on Sundays from Easter Day through the Day of Pentecost, on all the days of Easter Week, and on Ascension Day. It may be used at other times as desired, but not on Sundays or ordinary weekdays (that is, it may be used on major feast days) in Advent or Lent. Rite One restores the traditional medieval sequence of *Kyrie* and *Gloria* and allows the use of one or both; in Rite Two it is clear that one or the other is to be used. The *Gloria* or a suitable substitute is used to mark the festivity of great feasts, and it may be used at other times except for somber seasons of preparation. For these latter the somewhat more restrained praise of the *Kyrie* or *Trisagion* ("Holy God . . .") is appropriate.

The translation of the *Gloria* is that of ICET, and for extended comments the reader is referred to *Prayers We Have in Common* (2nd edition), pages 11-13. Since the text is neither a theological statement like the creeds, nor a biblical text (with the exception of the opening lines), the translators have taken some liberties with the original to reduce repetition and to clarify the structure. Their translation has been well received. Their translation of the *Kyrie* is shorter than the traditional one, and this brevity goes some distance to making it a shout of acclamation.

## The Collect of the Day

From time to time people have asked why the contemporary collects tell God things about himself which he already knows, as on Christmas Day, page 213, "Almighty God, you have given your only begotten Son . . ." This is simply a form of anamnesis, in that we remember before God one of his attributes or actions and because of that pray that he will do something. The relative clauses of the traditional forms did the same thing. Certainly no one would imagine that the prayer "Almighty God, who hast given us thy only-begotten Son to take our nature upon him" PBCP, page 161) is addressed to one particular God who is described by this phrase as against some other God "who in the Paschal mystery [has] established the new covenant of reconciliation" (PBCP, page 172).

The basic shape of the liturgy of the Word has been discussed in Rite One and does not need further comment. However, there are different forms for the Prayers of the People and Confession of Sin and a new version of the Nicene Creed. These deserve some comment.

## The Nicene Creed

The Creed and The Lord's Prayer are the two ICET translations which have caused the most discussion. In light of the many comments received they have been revised and refined. The translators describe their work on the Creed as "an attempt to achieve simplicity and clarity without losing any point of theological significance" (page 6). Although their work merits extensive comment, one point is most significant. The shift to "We" is a restoration of the original text as it was adopted in 381 at Constantinople. There is a distinction between the Apostles' Creed with its origin in the individual profession of faith made at Baptism and the Nicene Creed which expresses the common faith of the assembled Church. We belong to the community which describes its knowledge of God in these terms. As the Nicene Creed is more theological in content than the simple descriptive Apostles' Creed, it is appropriate that the theological consensus found there be expressed as "We believe."

## The Prayers of the People

The directions for the intercessions on page 359 are repeated and expanded on page 383 at the beginning of the suggested forms of prayers. In contrast to the prayer for the whole state of

Christ's Church and the World in Rite One, there is a great deal of freedom in the Rite Two intercessions. Certain things should be prayed for at any public celebration. At a marriage or burial, or in the event that baptisms are celebrated at a time other than a regular public service, prayers may be limited to the specific occasion; but with these possible exceptions, the objects of the Church's prayers should be those concerns listed in the directions for the prayers.

This is one point in the service where creativity and a high degree of spontaneity are in order and should be encouraged. One of the six forms printed on pages 383-395 may be used with suitable adaptations and insertions, but there is freedom to devise other forms as well. Some occasions will call for the more formal litanies of Forms I and V which are drawn from traditional Orthodox prayers. The dialogue style of Forms III and VI or the somewhat freer Form IV will be appropriate in other contexts. The informality and the directed silence of Form II can be used to great effect in certain intimate celebrations. It should be noted that in the various forms those petitions which have bars in the margin may be omitted. The freedom to experiment and to adapt should make the Prayers of the People one of the major points of the service.

This importance can be reinforced by the sensitive use of the concluding collect. There is, as indicated on page 394, a great deal of freedom in summarizing the prayers by the use of these options. For example, here could be placed the seasonal collects used in the 1928 book; that is, the Collects for the First Sunday of Advent or for Ash Wednesday, which were to be used after the Collect of the Day in their respective seasons, could be used here in the same way. There is no reason the practice should not also be extended to the festal seasons of Christmas and Easter.

**Confession of Sin**

Some of the forms of intercession (I, V, and VI) include optional requests for the forgiveness of the congregation's sins. These should not ordinarily be used when a Confession of Sin is to follow. As was suggested on page 18, there are times when the Confession might be omitted, but it is assumed that on most occasions the service will contain some form of Confession of Sin. The contemporary-language form of confession is matched by a new form of absolution which declares that God's mercy and forgiveness are ours through Christ, that we are strengthened by God in all goodness, and that the power of the Spirit keeps us in eternal life. The way this is structured around the persons of the Trinity, and the recognition that eternal life is our present possession, recover important theological points which the traditional form did not contain.

The discussion of the Peace in Rite One (page 18) applies equally well here. The Peace is at the center of the service. One might almost say it is the pivot around which the service revolves. The Proclamation of the Word of God reminds us of the Gospel which unites us in Christ, and the Celebration of the Holy Communion restores us to that unity. The Peace is a symbolic expression of this unity. It is not an interruption of the service, nor is it a time for idle chatter, but it is a pause during which we act out the unity which is ours.

## The Great Thanksgiving

With the shift from an understanding of this central point of the service as a prayer which merely consecrates the elements to an act of thanksgiving and praise in which the gifts and the congregation are made one with Christ, the way is opened for a greater freedom in the content and shape of the Eucharistic Prayer. There is no longer a narrow concentration on exactly what language is necessary to consecrate validly; rather it is felt that as long as the shape and stated intention is consistent with the past, great flexibility can be allowed. The four Eucharistic Prayers of Rite Two point to the kind of enrichment of eucharistic worship which is possible.

Each of these contemporary prayers has its own theological emphases, its own selection of biblical and symbolic imagery, and its own particular shape. They all contain, as does Eucharistic Prayer II of Rite One, the basic elements which characterize the "ideal" eucharistic prayer. They praise and thank God for creation, especially his creation of humanity in his image; for the way his love has been shown in history to his people; and for the Incarnation, death and resurrection of his Son. In this context the institution of the Eucharist is recalled, and the present celebration, the sacrifice of praise and thanksgiving, is offered as an anamnesis of Christ's redeeming acts. The Holy Spirit is invoked for the blessing upon the bread and wine, that they may be the Body and Blood of Christ, and upon the congregation, that they may show in their lives the fruits of their participation. A doxology concludes each prayer with praise to the Father, in and through the Son, in the unity of the Holy Spirit. This sums up the shape of the entire prayer in the final phrases and states the pattern for all Christian Prayer. The great AMEN at the conclusion signals the congregation's assent and its participation in the whole eucharistic action. Each of the prayers directs that in the midst of the prayer the congregation join with the celebrant in an acclamation of anamnesis. This is another way of showing their participation in the offering of the entire prayer.

Eucharistic Prayers A and B include the use of a Proper Preface which holds up one aspect of redemption appropriate to the season of the Church Year or other occasion. Prayers C and D do not provide such prefaces because they include a summary of what the annual cycle of proper prefaces contains.

Eucharistic Prayer D deserves a specific comment. It represents the work of a group of scholars drawn from the major American denominations who wanted to produce a prayer acceptable to all their churches. It is a revision of an ancient Greek eucharistic prayer ascribed to St. Basil, and it formed the basis for one of the new Roman Catholic eucharistic prayers. This is the longest one in the Proposed Book, but its length comes from the richness and variety of biblical imagery and not from much repetition. It is one of the gems of this book, and one hopes its length will not deter its occasional use.

The Lord's Prayer may be used in either the traditional translation or in a revised ICET version. The changes in the latter from the earlier trial services are in response to specific criticisms of the first versions and reflect the difficulty of accurate translation of something which is so familiar while its original meaning is so foreign. "Save us from the time of trial" expresses the fear of becoming apostate under torture more accurately than "Lead us not into temptation." Even if torture is not a common risk today, that kind of self-serving denial of faith is.

### The Breaking of the Bread

The comments at this point of Rite One (page 25ff) apply here as well. In line with the moderation of penitential material in Rite Two, the Prayer of Humble Access is deleted, and the *Agnus Dei* is not printed at this point. If desired, the latter may be substituted for "Christ our Passover," in the ICET version found on page 407.

For postcommunion devotions two prayers are provided. The first is a new prayer, and the second is a contemporary paraphrase of the prayer at this point in Rite One. They both ask that through participation in the sacrament, the members of the congregation may be strengthened for their mission to the world as ministers and witnesses to Christ.

The blessing is permitted, not required as in Rite One. Its omission has been encouraged because a simple priestly blessing is actually anticlimactic after the blessing of reception of Holy Communion. The forms in Rite One might be used, if any blessing is desired, or (and this is probably more appropriate) some blessing proper to the season might be used. The dismissals are the expected conclusion to the service; their major note is on the push out into the world to live out the implications of the entire service.

## Communion under Special Circumstances

Prayer Books since 1552 have had no provision for communion outside the context of complete, if abridged, celebrations of the Eucharist. The rubrics in the Communion of the Sick (BCP 1928, pages 321-323) provide for shortening the service when expedient, but such abbreviation still assumes that the elements are consecrated in the presence of those who will receive them. For many years, it has been customary for communion to be received by sick and shut-in persons from the reserved sacrament, but such a practice has been in violation of the rubrics. The form on pages 396-399 of the Proposed Book provides directions for how such communions are to be administered. The rubrics are clear enough to need no comment except to highlight the insistence that occasional full celebrations are still in order for shut-ins, and that when this form is used some scripture is to be read so that Christ's presence is experienced in both Word and Sacrament. Administration of Communion from the reserved sacrament is one of the traditional ministries of a deacon. The form of absolution used by a deacon is not the priestly declaration of forgiveness but a prayer which assumes that "God is faithful and just to forgive sins" for those who repent and confess.

## An Order for Celebrating the Holy Eucharist

Among the responses to the 1967 Liturgy of the Lord's Supper received by the Standing Liturgical Commission was a large number of requests that the Eucharist be made absolutely freeform. The Commission speaks, in *Prayer Book Studies* 25, page 25, of "groups of people of varying size and character who are searching for a living experience of worship outside of what, to them at least, appears as a rigid institutional framework." They ask in one way or another whether loyal membership in the Church and faithfulness to Christ's command to "do this for the remembrance of me" demand the use of an established order of service. Rite Three, as this order is usually called, is the Church's response to these questions.

The Proposed Book and the Church which adopted it says, "These are the elements essential to a celebration of the Eucharist." The rubrics intend to make sure that the members of the congregation at such informal services are prepared for and expect something different from regular public celebrations. In celebrations which conform to this outline, those who want less formal, more spontaneous services can find freedom to express their religious sense with the assurance that their worship is part of the worship offered to God by the Christian Church.

The two forms for the Great Thanksgiving provide the essential parts of a Christian eucharistic prayer while allowing the particular community to express much of what makes it unique. Although this order is not the normal public worship of the Church, most Episcopalians would find their participation of worship enriched by an occasional experience of worship in this form.

# The Holy Eucharist

The Liturgy for the
Proclamation of the Word of God and
Celebration of the Holy Communion

## An Exhortation

*This Exhortation may be used, in whole or in part, either during the Liturgy or at other times. In the absence of a deacon or priest, this Exhortation may be read by a lay person. The people stand or sit.*

Beloved in the Lord: Our Savior Christ, on the night before he suffered, instituted the Sacrament of his Body and Blood as a sign and pledge of his love, for the continual remembrance of the sacrifice of his death, and for a spiritual sharing in his risen life. For in these holy Mysteries we are made one with Christ, and Christ with us; we are made one body in him, and members one of another.

Having in mind, therefore, his great love for us, and in obedience to his command, his Church renders to Almighty God our heavenly Father never-ending thanks for the creation of the world, for his continual providence over us, for his love for all mankind, and for the redemption of the world by our Savior Christ, who took upon himself our flesh, and humbled himself even to death on the cross, that he might make us the children of God by the power of the Holy Spirit, and exalt us to everlasting life.

But if we are to share rightly in the celebration of those holy Mysteries, and be nourished by that spiritual Food, we must remember the dignity of that holy Sacrament. I therefore call upon you to consider how Saint Paul exhorts all persons to prepare themselves carefully before eating of that Bread and drinking of that Cup.

For, as the benefit is great, if with penitent hearts and living faith we receive the holy Sacrament, so is the danger great, if we receive it improperly, not recognizing the Lord's Body. Judge yourselves, therefore, lest you be judged by the Lord.

Examine your lives and conduct by the rule of God's commandments, that you may perceive wherein you have offended in what you have done or left undone, whether in thought, word, or deed. And acknowledge your sins before Almighty God, with full purpose of amendment of life, being ready to make restitution for all injuries and wrongs done by you to others; and also being ready to forgive those who have offended you, in order that you yourselves may be forgiven. And then, being reconciled with one another, come to the banquet of that most heavenly Food.

And if, in your preparation, you need help and counsel, then go and open your grief to a discreet and understanding priest, and confess your sins, that you may receive the benefit of absolution, and spiritual counsel and advice; to the removal of scruple and doubt, the assurance of pardon, and the strengthening of your faith.

To Christ our Lord who loves us, and washed us in his own blood, and made us a kingdom of priests to serve his God and Father, to him be glory in the Church evermore. Through him let us offer continually the sacrifice of praise, which is our bounden duty and service, and, with faith in him, come boldly before the throne of grace [and humbly confess our sins to Almighty God].

### The Decalogue: Traditional

God spake these words, and said:
I am the Lord thy God who brought thee out of the land of Egypt, out of the house of bondage. Thou shalt have none other gods but me.
*Lord, have mercy upon us,*
*and incline our hearts to keep this law.*

Thou shalt not make to thyself any graven image, nor the likeness of any thing that is in heaven above, or in the earth beneath, or in the water under the earth; thou shalt not bow down to them, nor worship them.
*Lord, have mercy upon us,*
*and incline our hearts to keep this law.*

Thou shalt not take the Name of the Lord thy God in vain.
*Lord, have mercy upon us,*
*and incline our hearts to keep this law.*

Remember that thou keep holy the Sabbath day.
*Lord, have mercy upon us,*
*and incline our hearts to keep this law.*

Honor thy father and thy mother.
*Lord, have mercy upon us,*
*and incline our hearts to keep this law.*

Thou shalt do no murder.
*Lord, have mercy upon us,*
*and incline our hearts to keep this law.*

Thou shalt not commit adultery.
*Lord, have mercy upon us,*
*and incline our hearts to keep this law.*

Thou shalt not steal.
*Lord, have mercy upon us,*
*and incline our hearts to keep this law.*

Thou shalt not bear false witness against thy neighbor.
*Lord, have mercy upon us,*
*and incline our hearts to keep this law.*

Thou shalt not covet.
*Lord, have mercy upon us,*
*and write all these thy laws in our hearts, we beseech thee.*

# A Penitential Order: Rite One

*For use at the beginning of the Liturgy, or as a separate service.*

*A hymn, psalm, or anthem may be sung.*

*The people standing, the Celebrant says*

           Blessed be God: Father, Son, and Holy Spirit.
*People*    And blessed be his kingdom, now and for ever. Amen.

*In place of the above, from Easter Day through the Day of Pentecost*

*Celebrant*  Alleluia. Christ is risen.
*People*      The Lord is risen indeed. Alleluia.

*In Lent and on other penitential occasions*

*Celebrant*  Bless the Lord who forgiveth all our sins;
*People*      His mercy endureth for ever.

*When used as a separate service, the Exhortation, page 316, may be read, or a homily preached.*

*The Decalogue, page 317, may be said, the people kneeling.*

*The Celebrant may read one of the following sentences*

Hear what our Lord Jesus Christ saith:
Thou shalt love the Lord thy God with all thy heart, and with all thy soul, and with all thy mind. This is the first and great commandment. And the second is like unto it: Thou shalt love thy neighbor as thyself. On these two commandments hang all the Law and the Prophets.    *Matthew 22:37-40*

If we say that we have no sin, we deceive ourselves, and the truth is not in us; but if we confess our sins, God is faithful and just to forgive us our sins, and to cleanse us from all unrighteousness.   *1 John 1:8, 9*

Seeing that we have a great high priest, that is passed into the heavens, Jesus the Son of God, let us come boldly unto the throne of grace, that we may obtain mercy, and find grace to help in time of need.   *Hebrews 4:14, 16*

*The Deacon or Celebrant then says*

Let us humbly confess our sins unto Almighty God.

*Silence may be kept.*

*Minister and People*

Most merciful God,
we confess that we have sinned against thee
in thought, word, and deed,
by what we have done,
and by what we have left undone.
We have not loved thee with our whole heart;
we have not loved our neighbors as ourselves.
We are truly sorry and we humbly repent.
For the sake of thy Son Jesus Christ,
have mercy on us and forgive us;
that we may delight in thy will,
and walk in thy ways,
to the glory of thy Name. Amen.

*or this*

Almighty and most merciful Father,
we have erred and strayed from thy ways like lost sheep,
we have followed too much the devices and desires of our
    own hearts,

we have offended against thy holy laws,
we have left undone those things which we ought to
   have done,
and we have done those things which we ought not to
   have done.
But thou, O Lord, have mercy upon us,
spare thou those who confess their faults,
restore thou those who are penitent,
according to thy promises declared unto mankind
in Christ Jesus our Lord;
and grant, O most merciful Father, for his sake,
that we may hereafter live a godly, righteous, and sober life,
to the glory of thy holy Name. Amen.

*The Bishop when present, or the Priest, stands and says*

The Almighty and merciful Lord grant you absolution and remission of all your sins, true repentance, amendment of life, and the grace and consolation of his Holy Spirit. *Amen.*

*A deacon or lay person using the preceding form substitutes "us" for "you" and "our" for "your."*

*When this Order is used at the beginning of the Liturgy, the service continues with the Kyrie eleison, the Trisagion, or the Gloria in excelsis.*

*When used separately, it concludes with suitable prayers, and the Grace or a blessing.*

# Concerning the Celebration

It is the bishop's prerogative, when present, to be the principal celebrant at the Lord's Table, and to preach the Gospel.

At all celebrations of the Liturgy, it is fitting that the principal celebrant, whether bishop or priest, be assisted by other priests, and by deacons and lay persons.

It is appropriate that the other priests present stand with the celebrant at the Altar, and join in the consecration of the gifts, in breaking the Bread, and in distributing Communion.

A deacon should read the Gospel and may lead the Prayers of the People. Deacons should also serve at the Lord's Table, preparing and placing on it the offerings of bread and wine, and assisting in the ministration of the Sacrament to the people. In the absence of a deacon, these duties may be performed by an assisting priest.

Lay persons appointed by the celebrant should normally be assigned the reading of the Lessons which precede the Gospel, and may lead the Prayers of the People.

Morning or Evening Prayer may be used in place of all that precedes the Peace and the Offertory, provided that a lesson from the Gospel is always included, and that the intercessions conform to the directions given for the Prayers of the People.

Additional Directions are on page 406.

# The Holy Eucharist: Rite One

## The Word of God

*A hymn, psalm, or anthem may be sung.*

*The people standing, the Celebrant may say*

              Blessed be God: Father, Son, and Holy Spirit.
*People*    And blessed be his kingdom, now and for ever. Amen.

*In place of the above, from Easter Day through the Day of Pentecost*

*Celebrant*  Alleluia. Christ is risen.
*People*     The Lord is risen indeed. Alleluia.

*In Lent and on other penitential occasions*

*Celebrant*  Bless the Lord who forgiveth all our sins;
*People*     His mercy endureth for ever.

*The Celebrant says*

Almighty God, unto whom all hearts are open, all desires known, and from whom no secrets are hid: Cleanse the thoughts of our hearts by the inspiration of thy Holy Spirit, that we may perfectly love thee, and worthily magnify thy holy Name; through Christ our Lord. *Amen.*

*Then the Ten Commandments (page 317) may be said, or the following*

Hear what our Lord Jesus Christ saith:
Thou shalt love the Lord thy God with all thy heart, and with all thy soul, and with all thy mind. This is the first and great commandment. And the second is like unto it: Thou shalt love thy neighbor as thyself. On these two commandments hang all the Law and the Prophets.

*Here is sung or said*

| Lord, have mercy upon us. | | Kyrie eleison. |
| *Christ, have mercy upon us.* | *or* | *Christe eleison.* |
| Lord, have mercy upon us. | | Kyrie eleison. |

*or this*

Holy God,
Holy and Mighty,
Holy Immortal One,
*Have mercy upon us.*

*When appointed, the following hymn or some other song of praise is sung or said, in addition to, or in place of, the preceding, all standing*

Glory be to God on high,
 and on earth peace, good will towards men.

We praise thee, we bless thee,
 we worship thee,
 we glorify thee,
 we give thanks to thee for thy great glory,
O Lord God, heavenly King, God the Father Almighty.

O Lord, the only-begotten Son, Jesus Christ;
O Lord God, Lamb of God, Son of the Father,
 that takest away the sins of the world,
 have mercy upon us.

Thou that takest away the sins of the world,
    receive our prayer.
Thou that sittest at the right hand of God the Father,
    have mercy upon us.

For thou only art holy;
thou only art the Lord;
thou only, O Christ,
    with the Holy Ghost,
    art most high in the glory of God the Father. Amen.

## The Collect of the Day

*The Celebrant says to the people*

> The Lord be with you.
*People*   And with thy spirit.
*Celebrant*  Let us pray.

*The Celebrant says the Collect.*

*People*   Amen.

## The Lessons

*The people sit. One or two Lessons, as appointed, are read, the Reader first saying*

A Reading (Lesson) from _____.

*A citation giving chapter and verse may be added.*

*After each Reading, the Reader may say*

> The Word of the Lord.
*People*   Thanks be to God.

*or the Reader may say*   Here endeth the Reading (Epistle).

*Silence may follow.*

*A Psalm, hymn, or anthem may follow each Reading.*

*Then, all standing, the Deacon or a Priest reads the Gospel, first saying*

    The Holy Gospel of our Lord Jesus Christ
    according to ―――――.
*People*   Glory be to thee, O Lord.

*After the Gospel, the Reader says*

    The Gospel of the Lord.
*People*   Praise be to thee, O Christ.

## The Sermon

*On Sundays and other Major Feasts there follows, all standing*

## The Nicene Creed

We believe in one God,
    the Father, the Almighty,
    maker of heaven and earth,
    of all that is, seen and unseen.

We believe in one Lord, Jesus Christ,
    the only Son of God,
    eternally begotten of the Father,
    God from God, Light from Light,
    true God from true God,
    begotten, not made,
    of one Being with the Father.
    Through him all things were made.
    For us and for our salvation
        he came down from heaven:

by the power of the Holy Spirit
> he became incarnate from the Virgin Mary,
> and was made man.
For our sake he was crucified under Pontius Pilate;
> he suffered death and was buried.
> On the third day he rose again
>> in accordance with the Scriptures;
> he ascended into heaven
>> and is seated at the right hand of the Father.
He will come again in glory to judge the living and the dead,
> and his kingdom will have no end.

We believe in the Holy Spirit, the Lord, the giver of life,
> who proceeds from the Father and the Son.
> With the Father and the Son he is worshiped and glorified.
> He has spoken through the Prophets.
> We believe in one holy catholic and apostolic Church.
> We acknowledge one baptism for the forgiveness of sins.
> We look for the resurrection of the dead,
>> and the life of the world to come. Amen.

*or this*

I believe in one God,
> the Father Almighty,
> maker of heaven and earth,
> and of all things visible and invisible;

And in one Lord Jesus Christ,
> the only-begotten Son of God,
> begotten of his Father before all worlds,
> God of God, Light of Light,
> very God of very God,
> begotten, not made,
> being of one substance with the Father;
> by whom all things were made;

who for us men and for our salvation
  came down from heaven,
and was incarnate by the Holy Ghost of the Virgin Mary,
  and was made man;
and was crucified also for us under Pontius Pilate;
he suffered and was buried;
and the third day he rose again according to the Scriptures,
and ascended into heaven,
and sitteth on the right hand of the Father;
and he shall come again, with glory,
  to judge both the quick and the dead;
whose kingdom shall have no end.

And I believe in the Holy Ghost the Lord, and Giver of Life,
  who proceedeth from the Father and the Son;
  who with the Father and the Son together is worshiped
    and glorified;
  who spake by the Prophets.
And I believe one holy Catholic and Apostolic Church;
I acknowledge one Baptism for the remission of sins;
and I look for the resurrection of the dead,
  and the life of the world to come. Amen.

### The Prayers of the People

*Intercession is offered according to the following form, or in accordance with the directions on page 383.*

*The Deacon or other person appointed says*

Let us pray for the whole state of Christ's Church and the world.

*After each paragraph of this prayer, the People may make an appropriate response, as directed.*

Almighty and everliving God, who in thy holy Word hast taught us to make prayers, and supplications, and to give thanks for all men: Receive these our prayers which we offer unto thy divine Majesty, beseeching thee to inspire continually the Universal Church with the spirit of truth, unity, and concord; and grant that all those who do confess thy holy Name may agree in the truth of thy holy Word, and live in unity and godly love.

Give grace, O heavenly Father, to all bishops and other ministers [especially _____], that they may, both by their life and doctrine, set forth thy true and lively Word, and rightly and duly administer thy holy Sacraments.

And to all thy people give thy heavenly grace, and especially to this congregation here present; that, with meek heart and due reverence, they may hear and receive thy holy Word, truly serving thee in holiness and righteousness all the days of their life.

We beseech thee also so to rule the hearts of those who bear the authority of government in this and every land [especially _____], that they may be led to wise decisions and right actions for the welfare and peace of the world.

Open, O Lord, the eyes of all people to behold thy gracious hand in all thy works, that, rejoicing in thy whole creation, they may honor thee with their substance, and be faithful stewards of thy bounty.

And we most humbly beseech thee, of thy goodness, O Lord, to comfort and succor [_____ and] all those who, in this transitory life, are in trouble, sorrow, need, sickness, or any other adversity.

*Additional petitions and thanksgivings may be included here.*

And we also bless thy holy Name for all thy servants departed this life in thy faith and fear [especially _____], beseeching thee to grant them continual growth in thy love and service; and to grant us grace so to follow the good examples of [_____ and of] all thy saints, that with them we may be partakers of thy heavenly kingdom.

Grant these our prayers, O Father, for Jesus Christ's sake, our only Mediator and Advocate. *Amen.*

*If there is no celebration of the Communion, or if a priest is not available, the service is concluded as directed on page 406.*

## Confession of Sin

*A Confession of Sin is said here if it has not been said earlier. On occasion, the Confession may be omitted.*

*The Deacon or Celebrant says the following, or else the Exhortation on page 316*

Ye who do truly and earnestly repent you of your sins, and are in love and charity with your neighbors, and intend to lead a new life, following the commandments of God, and walking from henceforth in his holy ways: Draw near with faith, and make your humble confession to Almighty God, devoutly kneeling.

*or this*

Let us humbly confess our sins unto Almighty God.

*Silence may be kept.*

*Minister and People*
Almighty God,
Father of our Lord Jesus Christ,
maker of all things, judge of all men:
We acknowledge and bewail our manifold sins
    and wickedness,
which we from time to time most grievously have committed,
by thought, word, and deed, against thy divine Majesty,
provoking most justly thy wrath and indignation against us.
We do earnestly repent,
and are heartily sorry for these our misdoings;
the remembrance of them is grievous unto us,
the burden of them is intolerable.
Have mercy upon us,
have mercy upon us, most merciful Father;
for thy Son our Lord Jesus Christ's sake,
forgive us all that is past;
and grant that we may ever hereafter
serve and please thee in newness of life,
to the honor and glory of thy Name;
through Jesus Christ our Lord. Amen.

*or this*
Most merciful God,
we confess that we have sinned against thee
in thought, word, and deed,
by what we have done,
and by what we have left undone.
We have not loved thee with our whole heart;
we have not loved our neighbors as ourselves.
We are truly sorry and we humbly repent.
For the sake of thy Son Jesus Christ,
have mercy on us and forgive us;
that we may delight in thy will,
and walk in thy ways,
to the glory of thy Name. Amen.

*The Bishop when present, or the Priest, stands and says*

Almighty God, our heavenly Father, who of his great mercy hath promised forgiveness of sins to all those who with hearty repentance and true faith turn unto him, have mercy upon you, pardon and deliver you from all your sins, confirm and strengthen you in all goodness, and bring you to everlasting life; through Jesus Christ our Lord. *Amen.*

*A Minister may then say one or more of the following sentences, first saying*

Hear the Word of God to all who truly turn to him.

Come unto me, all ye that travail and are heavy laden, and I will refresh you.   *Matthew 11:28*

God so loved the world, that he gave his only-begotten Son, to the end that all that believe in him should not perish, but have everlasting life.   *John 3:16*

This is a true saying, and worthy of all men to be received, that Christ Jesus came into the world to save sinners.
*1 Timothy 1:15*

If any man sin, we have an Advocate with the Father, Jesus Christ the righteous; and he is the perfect offering for our sins, and not for ours only, but for the sins of the whole world.   *1 John 2:1-2*

## The Peace

*All stand. The Celebrant says to the people*

        The peace of the Lord be always with you.
*People*    And with thy spirit.

*Then the Ministers and People may greet one another in the name of the Lord.*

# The Holy Communion

*The Celebrant may begin the Offertory with one of the sentences on pages 343-344, or with some other sentence of Scripture.*

*During the Offertory, a hymn, psalm, or anthem may be sung.*

*Representatives of the congregation bring the people's offerings of bread and wine, and money or other gifts, to the deacon or celebrant. The people stand while the offerings are presented and placed on the Altar.*

## The Great Thanksgiving

*An alternative form will be found on page 340.*

### Eucharistic Prayer I

*The people remain standing. The Celebrant, whether bishop or priest, faces them and sings or says*

         The Lord be with you.
*People*    And with thy spirit.
*Celebrant*  Lift up your hearts.
*People*    We lift them up unto the Lord.
*Celebrant*  Let us give thanks unto our Lord God.
*People*    It is meet and right so to do.

*Then, facing the Holy Table, the Celebrant proceeds*

It is very meet, right, and our bounden duty, that we should at all times, and in all places, give thanks unto thee, O Lord, holy Father, almighty, everlasting God.

*Here a Proper Preface is sung or said on all Sundays, and on other occasions as appointed.*

Therefore with Angels and Archangels, and with all the company of heaven, we laud and magnify thy glorious Name; evermore praising thee, and saying,

*Celebrant and People*

Holy, holy, holy, Lord God of Hosts:
Heaven and earth are full of thy glory.
Glory be to thee, O Lord Most High.

*Here may be added*

Blessed is he that cometh in the name of the Lord.
Hosanna in the highest.

*The people kneel or stand.*

*Then the Celebrant continues*

All glory be to thee, Almighty God, our heavenly Father, for that thou, of thy tender mercy, didst give thine only Son Jesus Christ to suffer death upon the cross for our redemption; who made there, by his one oblation of himself once offered, a full, perfect, and sufficient sacrifice, oblation, and satisfaction, for the sins of the whole world; and did institute, and in his holy Gospel command us to continue, a perpetual memory of that his precious death and sacrifice, until his coming again.

*At the following words concerning the bread, the Celebrant is to hold it, or lay a hand upon it; and at the words concerning the cup, to hold or place a hand upon the cup and any other vessel containing wine to be consecrated*

For in the night in which he was betrayed, he took bread; and when he had given thanks, he brake it, and gave it to his disciples, saying, "Take, eat, this is my Body, which is given for you. Do this in remembrance of me."

Likewise, after supper, he took the cup; and when he had given thanks, he gave it to them, saying, "Drink ye all of this; for this is my Blood of the New Testament, which is shed for you, and for many, for the remission of sins. Do this, as oft as ye shall drink it, in remembrance of me."

Wherefore, O Lord and heavenly Father, according to the institution of thy dearly beloved Son our Savior Jesus Christ, we, thy humble servants, do celebrate and make here before thy divine Majesty, with these thy holy gifts, which we now offer unto thee, the memorial thy Son hath commanded us to make; having in remembrance his blessed passion and precious death, his mighty resurrection and glorious ascension; rendering unto thee most hearty thanks for the innumerable benefits procured unto us by the same.

And we most humbly beseech thee, O merciful Father, to hear us; and, of thy almighty goodness, vouchsafe to bless and sanctify, with thy Word and Holy Spirit, these thy gifts and creatures of bread and wine; that we, receiving them according to thy Son our Savior Jesus Christ's holy institution, in remembrance of his death and passion, may be partakers of his most blessed Body and Blood.

And we earnestly desire thy fatherly goodness mercifully to accept this our sacrifice of praise and thanksgiving; most humbly beseeching thee to grant that, by the merits and death of thy Son Jesus Christ, and through faith in his blood, we, and all thy whole Church, may obtain remission of our sins, and all other benefits of his passion.

And here we offer and present unto thee, O Lord, our selves, our souls and bodies, to be a reasonable, holy, and living sacrifice unto thee; humbly beseeching thee that we, and all others who shall be partakers of this Holy Communion, may worthily receive the most precious Body and Blood of thy Son Jesus Christ, be filled with thy grace and heavenly benediction, and made one body with him, that he may dwell in us, and we in him.

And although we are unworthy, through our manifold sins, to offer unto thee any sacrifice, yet we beseech thee to accept this our bounden duty and service, not weighing our merits, but pardoning our offenses, through Jesus Christ our Lord;

By whom, and with whom, in the unity of the Holy Ghost, all honor and glory be unto thee, O Father Almighty, world without end. AMEN.

And now, as our Savior Christ hath taught us, we are bold to say,

*People and Celebrant*

Our Father, who art in heaven,
   hallowed be thy Name,
   thy kingdom come,
   thy will be done,
      on earth as it is in heaven.
Give us this day our daily bread.
And forgive us our trespasses,
   as we forgive those who trespass against us.
And lead us not into temptation,
   but deliver us from evil.
For thine is the kingdom, and the power, and the glory,
   for ever and ever. Amen.

## The Breaking of the Bread

*The Celebrant breaks the consecrated Bread.*

*A period of silence is kept.*

*Then may be sung or said*

[Alleluia.] Christ our Passover is sacrificed for us;
Therefore let us keep the feast. [Alleluia.]

*In Lent, Alleluia is omitted, and may be omitted at other times except during Easter Season.*

*The following or some other suitable anthem may be sung or said here*

O Lamb of God, that takest away the sins of the world,
have mercy upon us.
O Lamb of God, that takest away the sins of the world,
have mercy upon us.
O Lamb of God, that takest away the sins of the world,
grant us thy peace.

*The following prayer may be said. The People may join in saying this prayer*

We do not presume to come to this thy Table, O merciful Lord, trusting in our own righteousness, but in thy manifold and great mercies. We are not worthy so much as to gather up the crumbs under thy Table. But thou art the same Lord whose property is always to have mercy. Grant us therefore, gracious Lord, so to eat the flesh of thy dear Son Jesus Christ, and to drink his blood, that we may evermore dwell in him, and he in us. *Amen.*

*Facing the people, the Celebrant may say the following Invitation*

The Gifts of God for the People of God.

*and may add*   Take them in remembrance that Christ died for you, and feed on him in your hearts by faith, with thanksgiving.

*The ministers receive the Sacrament in both kinds, and then immediately deliver it to the people.*

*The Bread and the Cup are given to the communicants with these words*

The Body of our Lord Jesus Christ, which was given for thee, preserve thy body and soul unto everlasting life. Take and eat this in remembrance that Christ died for thee, and feed on him in thy heart by faith, with thanksgiving.

The Blood of our Lord Jesus Christ, which was shed for thee, preserve thy body and soul unto everlasting life. Drink this in remembrance that Christ's Blood was shed for thee, and be thankful.

*or with these words*

The Body (Blood) of our Lord Jesus Christ keep you in everlasting life. [*Amen.*]

*or with these words*

The Body of Christ, the bread of heaven. [*Amen.*]
The Blood of Christ, the cup of salvation. [*Amen.*]

*During the ministration of Communion, hymns, psalms, or anthems may be sung.*

*When necessary, the Celebrant consecrates additional bread and wine, using the form on page 408.*

*After Communion, the Celebrant says*

Let us pray.

*The People may join in saying this prayer*

Almighty and everliving God, we most heartily thank thee for that thou dost feed us, in these holy mysteries, with the spiritual food of the most precious Body and Blood of thy Son our Savior Jesus Christ; and dost assure us thereby of thy favor and goodness towards us; and that we are very members incorporate in the mystical body of thy Son, the blessed company of all faithful people; and are also heirs, through hope, of thy everlasting kingdom. And we humbly beseech thee, O heavenly Father, so to assist us with thy grace, that we may continue in that holy fellowship, and do all such good works as thou hast prepared for us to walk in; through Jesus Christ our Lord, to whom, with thee and the Holy Ghost, be all honor and glory, world without end. *Amen.*

*The Bishop when present, or the Priest, gives the blessing*

The peace of God, which passeth all understanding, keep your hearts and minds in the knowledge and love of God, and of his Son Jesus Christ our Lord; and the blessing of God Almighty, the Father, the Son, and the Holy Ghost, be amongst you, and remain with you always. *Amen.*

*or this*

The blessing of God Almighty, the Father, the Son, and the Holy Spirit, be upon you and remain with you for ever. *Amen.*

*The Deacon, or the Celebrant, may dismiss the people with these words*

         Let us go forth in the name of Christ.
*People*    Thanks be to God.

*or the following*

*Holy Eucharist I*

| | |
|---|---|
| *Deacon* | Go in peace to love and serve the Lord. |
| *People* | Thanks be to God. |

*or this*

| | |
|---|---|
| *Deacon* | Let us go forth into the world, rejoicing in the power of the Spirit. |
| *People* | Thanks be to God. |

*or this*

| | |
|---|---|
| *Deacon* | Let us bless the Lord. |
| *People* | Thanks be to God. |

*From the Easter Vigil through the Day of Pentecost "Alleluia, alleluia" may be added to any of the dismissals.*

*The People respond*   Thanks be to God. Alleluia, alleluia.


# Alternative Form of the Great Thanksgiving

### Eucharistic Prayer II

*The people remain standing. The Celebrant, whether bishop or priest, faces them and sings or says*

| | |
|---|---|
| | The Lord be with you. |
| *People* | And with thy spirit. |
| *Celebrant* | Lift up your hearts: |
| *People* | We lift them up unto the Lord. |
| *Celebrant* | Let us give thanks unto our Lord God. |
| *People* | It is meet and right so to do. |

*Then, facing the Holy Table, the Celebrant proceeds*

It is very meet, right, and our bounden duty, that we should at all times, and in all places, give thanks unto thee, O Lord, holy Father, almighty, everlasting God.

*Here a Proper Preface is sung or said on all Sundays, and on other occasions as appointed.*

Therefore with Angels and Archangels, and with all the company of heaven, we laud and magnify thy glorious Name; evermore praising thee, and saying,

*Celebrant and People*

Holy, holy, holy, Lord God of Hosts:
Heaven and earth are full of thy glory.
Glory be to thee, O Lord Most High.

*Here may be added*

Blessed is he that cometh in the name of the Lord.
Hosanna in the highest.

*The People kneel or stand.*

*Then the Celebrant continues*

All glory be to thee, O Lord our God, for that thou didst create heaven and earth, and didst make us in thine own image; and, of thy tender mercy, didst give thine only Son Jesus Christ to take our nature upon him, and to suffer death upon the cross for our redemption. He made there a full and perfect sacrifice for the whole world; and did institute, and in his holy Gospel command us to continue, a perpetual memory of that his precious death and sacrifice, until his coming again.

*At the following words concerning the bread, the Celebrant is to hold it, or lay a hand upon it; and at the words concerning the cup, to hold or place a hand upon the cup and any other vessel containing wine to be consecrated.*

For in the night in which he was betrayed, he took bread; and when he had given thanks to thee, he broke it, and gave it to his disciples, saying, "Take, eat, this is my Body, which is given for you. Do this in remembrance of me."

Likewise, after supper, he took the cup; and when he had given thanks, he gave it to them, saying, "Drink this, all of you; for this is my Blood of the New Covenant, which is shed for you, and for many, for the remission of sins. Do this, as oft as ye shall drink it, in remembrance of me."

Wherefore, O Lord and heavenly Father, we thy people do celebrate and make, with these thy holy gifts which we now offer unto thee, the memorial thy Son hath commanded us to make; having in remembrance his blessed passion and precious death, his mighty resurrection and glorious ascension; and looking for his coming again with power and great glory.

And we most humbly beseech thee, O merciful Father, to hear us, and, with thy Word and Holy Spirit, to bless and sanctify these gifts of bread and wine, that they may be unto us the Body and Blood of thy dearly-beloved Son Jesus Christ.

And we earnestly desire thy fatherly goodness to accept this our sacrifice of praise and thanksgiving, whereby we offer and present unto thee, O Lord, our selves, our souls and bodies. Grant, we beseech thee, that all who partake of this Holy Communion may worthily receive the most precious Body and Blood of thy Son Jesus Christ, and be filled with thy grace and heavenly benediction; and also that we and all thy whole Church may be made one body with him, that he may dwell in us, and we in him; through the same Jesus Christ our Lord;

By whom, and with whom, and in whom, in the unity of the Holy Ghost all honor and glory be unto thee, O Father Almighty, world without end. *AMEN.*

And now, as our Savior Christ hath taught us, we are bold to say,

*Continue with the Lord's Prayer, page 336.*

# Offertory Sentences

*One of the following, or some other appropriate sentence of Scripture, may be used*

Offer to God a sacrifice of thanksgiving, and make good thy vows unto the Most High.   *Psalm 50:14*

Ascribe to the Lord the honor due his Name; bring offerings and come into his courts.   *Psalm 96:8*

Walk in love, as Christ loved us and gave himself for us, an offering and sacrifice to God.   *Ephesians 5:2*

I beseech you, brethren, by the mercies of God, to present yourselves as a living sacrifice, holy and acceptable to God, which is your spiritual worship.   *Romans 12:1*

If thou bring thy gift to the altar, and there rememberest that thy brother hath aught against thee, leave there thy gift before the altar, and go thy way; first be reconciled to thy brother, and then come and offer thy gift.   *Matthew 5:23,24*

Through Christ let us continually offer to God the sacrifice of praise, that is, the fruit of lips that acknowledge his Name. But to do good and to distribute, forget not; for with such sacrifices God is well pleased.     *Hebrews 13:15,16*

Worthy art thou, O Lord our God, to receive glory and honor and power; for thou hast created all things, and by thy will they were created and have their being.     *Revelation 4:11*

Thine, O Lord, is the greatness, and the power, and the glory, and the victory, and the majesty. For all that is in the heaven and in the earth is thine. Thine is the kingdom, O Lord, and thou art exalted as head above all.     *1 Chronicles 29:11*

*or this bidding*

Let us with gladness present the offerings and oblations of our life and labor to the Lord.

# Proper Prefaces

**Preface of the Lord's Day**

*To be used on Sundays as appointed, but not on the succeeding weekdays*

### 1. Of God the Father

Creator of the light and source of life, who hast made us in thine image, and called us to new life in Jesus Christ our Lord.

*or the following*

2. *Of God the Son*

Through Jesus Christ our Lord; who on the first day of the week overcame death and the grave, and by his glorious resurrection opened to us the way of everlasting life.

*or this*

3. *Of God the Holy Spirit*

Who by water and the Holy Spirit hast made us a new people in Jesus Christ our Lord, to show forth thy glory in all the world.

**Prefaces for Seasons**

*To be used on Sundays and weekdays alike, except as otherwise appointed for Holy Days and Various Occasions*

*Advent*

Because thou didst send thy beloved Son to redeem us from sin and death, and to make us heirs in him of everlasting life; that when he shall come again in power and great triumph to judge the world, we may without shame or fear rejoice to behold his appearing.

*Incarnation*

Because thou didst give Jesus Christ, thine only Son, to be born for us; who, by the mighty power of the Holy Ghost, was made very Man of the substance of the Virgin Mary his mother; that we might be delivered from the bondage of sin, and receive power to become thy children.

*Epiphany*

Because in the mystery of the Word made flesh, thou hast caused a new light to shine in our hearts, to give the knowledge of thy glory in the face of thy Son Jesus Christ our Lord.

*Lent*

Through Jesus Christ our Lord, who was in every way tempted as we are, yet did not sin; by whose grace we are able to triumph over every evil, and to live no longer unto ourselves, but unto him who died for us and rose again.

*or this*

Who dost bid thy faithful people cleanse their hearts, and prepare with joy for the Paschal feast; that, fervent in prayer and in works of mercy, and renewed by thy Word and Sacraments, they may come to the fullness of grace which thou hast prepared for those who love thee.

*Holy Week*

Through Jesus Christ our Lord; who for our sins was lifted high upon the cross, that he might draw the whole world to himself; who by his suffering and death became the author of eternal salvation for all who put their trust in him.

*Easter*

But chiefly are we bound to praise thee for the glorious resurrection of thy Son Jesus Christ our Lord; for he is the very Paschal Lamb, who was sacrificed for us, and hath taken away the sin of the world; who by his death hath destroyed death, and by his rising to life again hath won for us everlasting life.

*Ascension*

Through thy dearly beloved Son Jesus Christ our Lord; who after his glorious resurrection manifestly appeared to his disciples; and in their sight ascended into heaven, to prepare a place for us; that where he is, there we might also be, and reign with him in glory.

*Pentecost*

Through Jesus Christ our Lord; according to whose true promise the Holy Ghost came down [on this day] from heaven, lighting upon the disciples, to teach them and to lead them into all truth; uniting peoples of many tongues in the confession of one faith, and giving to thy Church the power to serve thee as a royal priesthood, and to preach the gospel to all nations.

### Prefaces for Other Occasions

*Trinity Sunday*

For with thy co-eternal Son and Holy Spirit, thou art one God, one Lord, in Trinity of Persons and in Unity of Substance; and we celebrate the one and equal glory of thee, O Father, and of the Son, and of the Holy Spirit.

*All Saints*

Who, in the multitude of thy saints, hast compassed us about with so great a cloud of witnesses, that we, rejoicing in their fellowship, may run with patience the race that is set before us; and, together with them, may receive the crown of glory that fadeth not away.

*A Saint*

For the wonderful grace and virtue declared in all thy saints, who have been the chosen vessels of thy grace, and the lights of the world in their generations.

*or this*

Who in the obedience of thy saints hast given us an example of righteousness, and in their eternal joy a glorious pledge of the hope of our calling.

*or this*

Because thou art greatly glorified in the assembly of thy saints. All thy creatures praise thee, and thy faithful servants bless thee, confessing before the rulers of this world the great Name of thine only Son.

*Apostles and Ordinations*

Through the great shepherd of thy flock, Jesus Christ our Lord; who after his resurrection sent forth his apostles to preach the Gospel and to teach all nations; and promised to be with them always, even unto the end of the ages.

*Dedication of a Church*

Through Jesus Christ our great High Priest, in whom we are built up as living stones of a holy temple, that we might offer before thee a sacrifice of praise and prayer which is holy and pleasing in thy sight.

*Baptism*

Because in Jesus Christ our Lord thou hast received us as thy sons and daughters, made us citizens of thy kingdom, and given us the Holy Spirit to guide us into all truth.

*Marriage*

Because in the love of wife and husband, thou hast given us an image of the heavenly Jerusalem, adorned as a bride for her bridegroom, thy Son Jesus Christ our Lord; who loveth her and gave himself for her, that he might make the whole creation new.

*Commemoration of the Dead*

Through Jesus Christ our Lord; who rose victorious from the dead, and doth comfort us with the blessed hope of everlasting life; for to thy faithful people, O Lord, life is changed, not ended; and when our mortal body doth lie in death, there is prepared for us a dwelling place eternal in the heavens.

## The Decalogue: Contemporary

Hear the commandments of God to his people:
I am the Lord your God who brought you out of bondage.
You shall have no other gods but me.
*Amen. Lord have mercy.*

You shall not make for yourself any idol.
*Amen. Lord have mercy.*

You shall not invoke with malice the Name of the Lord your God.
*Amen. Lord have mercy.*

Remember the Sabbath Day and keep it holy.
*Amen. Lord have mercy.*

Honor your father and your mother.
*Amen. Lord have mercy.*

You shall not commit murder.
*Amen. Lord have mercy.*

You shall not commit adultery.
*Amen. Lord have mercy.*

You shall not steal.
*Amen. Lord have mercy.*

You shall not be a false witness.
*Amen. Lord have mercy.*

You shall not covet anything that belongs to your neighbor.
*Amen. Lord have mercy.*

# A Penitential Order: Rite Two

*For use at the beginning of the Liturgy, or as a separate service.*

*A hymn, psalm, or anthem may be sung.*

*The people standing, the Celebrant says*

          Blessed be God: Father, Son, and Holy Spirit.
*People*    And blessed be his kingdom, now and for ever. Amen.

*In place of the above, from Easter Day through the Day of Pentecost*

*Celebrant*  Alleluia. Christ is risen.
*People*      The Lord is risen indeed. Alleluia.

*In Lent and on other penitential occasions*

*Celebrant*  Bless the Lord who forgives all our sins;
*People*      His mercy endures for ever.

*When used as a separate service, the Exhortation, page 316, may be read, or a homily preached.*

*The Decalogue may be said, the people kneeling.*

*The Celebrant may read one of the following sentences*

Jesus said, "The first commandment is this: Hear, O Israel: The Lord our God is the only Lord. Love the Lord your God with all your heart, with all your soul, with all your mind, and with all your strength. The second is this: Love your neighbor as yourself. There is no other commandment greater than these."  *Mark 12:29-31*

If we say that we have no sin, we deceive ourselves, and the truth is not in us. But if we confess our sins, God, who is faithful and just, will forgive our sins and cleanse us from all unrighteousness.     *1 John 1:8,9*

Since we have a great high priest who has passed through the heavens, Jesus, the Son of God, let us with confidence draw near to the throne of grace, that we may receive mercy and find grace to help in time of need.     *Hebrews 4:14,16*

*The Deacon or Celebrant then says*

Let us confess our sins against God and our neighbor.

*Silence may be kept.*

*Minister and People*

Most merciful God,
we confess that we have sinned against you
in thought, word, and deed,
by what we have done,
and by what we have left undone.
We have not loved you with our whole heart;
we have not loved our neighbors as ourselves.
We are truly sorry and we humbly repent.
For the sake of your Son Jesus Christ,
have mercy on us and forgive us;
that we may delight in your will,
and walk in your ways,
to the glory of your Name. Amen.

*The Bishop when present, or the Priest, stands and says*

Almighty God have mercy on you, forgive you all your sins through our Lord Jesus Christ, strengthen you in all goodness, and by the power of the Holy Spirit keep you in eternal life. *Amen.*

*A deacon or lay person using the preceding form substitutes "us" for "you" and "our" for "your."*

*When this Order is used at the beginning of the Liturgy, the service continues with the Gloria in excelsis, the Kyrie eleison, or the Trisagion.*

*When used separately, it concludes with suitable prayers, and the Grace or a blessing.*

# Concerning the Celebration

It is the bishop's prerogative, when present, to be the principal celebrant at the Lord's Table, and to preach the Gospel.

At all celebrations of the Liturgy, it is fitting that the principal celebrant, whether bishop or priest, be assisted by other priests, and by deacons and lay persons.

It is appropriate that the other priests present stand with the celebrant at the Altar, and join in the consecration of the gifts, in breaking the Bread, and in distributing Communion.

A deacon should read the Gospel and may lead the Prayers of the People. Deacons should also serve at the Lord's Table, preparing and placing on it the offerings of bread and wine, and assisting in the ministration of the Sacrament to the people. In the absence of a deacon, these duties may be performed by an assisting priest.

Lay persons appointed by the celebrant should normally be assigned the reading of the Lessons which precede the Gospel, and may lead the Prayers of the People.

Morning or Evening Prayer may be used in place of all that precedes the Peace and the Offertory, provided that a lesson from the Gospel is always included, and that the intercessions conform to the directions given for the Prayers of the People.

Additional Directions are on page 406.

# The Holy Eucharist: Rite Two

## The Word of God

*A hymn, psalm, or anthem may be sung.*

*The people standing, the Celebrant says*

              Blessed be God: Father, Son, and Holy Spirit.
*People*    And blessed be his kingdom, now and for ever. Amen.

*In place of the above, from Easter Day through the Day of Pentecost*

*Celebrant*  Alleluia. Christ is risen.
*People*     The Lord is risen indeed. Alleluia.

*In Lent and on other penitential occasions*

*Celebrant*  Bless the Lord who forgives all our sins;
*People*     His mercy endures for ever.

*The Celebrant may say*

Almighty God, to you all hearts are open, all desires known, and from you no secrets are hid: Cleanse the thoughts of our hearts by the inspiration of your Holy Spirit, that we may perfectly love you, and worthily magnify your holy Name; through Christ our Lord. *Amen.*

*When appointed, the following hymn or some other song of praise is sung or said, all standing*

Glory to God in the highest,
    and peace to his people on earth.

Lord God, heavenly King,
almighty God and Father,
    we worship you, we give you thanks,
    we praise you for your glory.

Lord Jesus Christ, only Son of the Father,
Lord God, Lamb of God,
you take away the sin of the world:
    have mercy on us;
you are seated at the right hand of the Father:
    receive our prayer.

For you alone are the Holy One,
you alone are the Lord,
you alone are the Most High,
    Jesus Christ,
    with the Holy Spirit,
    in the glory of God the Father. Amen.

*On other occasions the following is used*

| | | |
|---|---|---|
| Lord, have mercy. | | Kyrie eleison. |
| *Christ, have mercy.* | or | *Christe eleison.* |
| Lord, have mercy. | | Kyrie eleison. |

*or this*

Holy God,
Holy and Mighty,
Holy Immortal One,
*Have mercy upon us.*

## The Collect of the Day

*The Celebrant says to the people*

>The Lord be with you.
*People*   And also with you.
*Celebrant*   Let us pray.

*The Celebrant says the Collect.*

*People*   Amen.

## The Lessons

*The people sit. One or two Lessons, as appointed, are read, the Reader first saying*

A Reading (Lesson) from _____.

*A citation giving chapter and verse may be added.*

*After each Reading, the Reader may say*

>The Word of the Lord.
*People*   Thanks be to God.

*or the Reader may say*   Here ends the Reading (Epistle).

*Silence may follow.*

*A Psalm, hymn, or anthem may follow each Reading.*

*Then, all standing, the Deacon or a Priest reads the Gospel, first saying*

>The Holy Gospel of our Lord Jesus Christ according to _____.
*People*   Glory to you, Lord Christ.

*After the Gospel, the Reader says*

          The Gospel of the Lord.
*People*    Praise to you, Lord Christ.

## The Sermon

*On Sundays and other Major Feasts there follows, all standing*

## The Nicene Creed

We believe in one God,
   the Father, the Almighty,
   maker of heaven and earth,
   of all that is, seen and unseen.

We believe in one Lord, Jesus Christ,
   the only Son of God,
   eternally begotten of the Father,
   God from God, Light from Light,
   true God from true God,
   begotten, not made,
   of one Being with the Father.
   Through him all things were made.
   For us and for our salvation
      he came down from heaven:
   by the power of the Holy Spirit
      he became incarnate from the Virgin Mary,
      and was made man.
   For our sake he was crucified under Pontius Pilate;
      he suffered death and was buried.
      On the third day he rose again
         in accordance with the Scriptures;
      he ascended into heaven
         and is seated at the right hand of the Father.

He will come again in glory to judge the living and the dead,
    and his kingdom will have no end.
We believe in the Holy Spirit, the Lord, the giver of life,
    who proceeds from the Father and the Son.
    With the Father and the Son he is worshiped and glorified.
    He has spoken through the Prophets.
    We believe in one holy catholic and apostolic Church.
    We acknowledge one baptism for the forgiveness of sins.
    We look for the resurrection of the dead,
        and the life of the world to come. Amen.

## The Prayers of the People

*Prayer is offered with intercession for*

*The Universal Church, its members, and its mission*
*The Nation and all in authority*
*The welfare of the world*
*The concerns of the local community*
*Those who suffer and those in any trouble*
*The departed (with commemoration of a saint when appropriate)*

*See the forms beginning on page 383.*

*If there is no celebration of the Communion, or if a priest is not available, the service is concluded as directed on page 406.*

## Confession of Sin

*A Confession of Sin is said here if it has not been said earlier. On occasion, the Confession may be omitted.*

*One of the sentences from the Penitential Order on page 351 may be said.*

*The Deacon or Celebrant says*

Let us confess our sins against God and our neighbor.

*Silence may be kept.*

*Minister and People*

Most merciful God,
we confess that we have sinned against you
in thought, word, and deed,
by what we have done,
and by what we have left undone.
We have not loved you with our whole heart;
we have not loved our neighbors as ourselves.
We are truly sorry and we humbly repent.
For the sake of your Son Jesus Christ,
have mercy on us and forgive us;
that we may delight in your will,
and walk in your ways,
to the glory of your Name. Amen.

*The Bishop when present, or the Priest, stands and says*

Almighty God have mercy on you, forgive you all your sins through our Lord Jesus Christ, strengthen you in all goodness, and by the power of the Holy Spirit keep you in eternal life. *Amen.*

## The Peace

*All stand. The Celebrant says to the people*

          The peace of the Lord be always with you.
*People*    And also with you.

*Then the Ministers and People may greet one another in the name of the Lord.*

# The Holy Communion

*The Celebrant may begin the Offertory with one of the sentences on page 376, or with some other sentence of Scripture.*

*During the Offertory, a hymn, psalm, or anthem may be sung.*

*Representatives of the congregation bring the people's offerings of bread and wine, and money or other gifts, to the deacon or celebrant. The people stand while the offerings are presented and placed on the Altar.*

## The Great Thanksgiving

*Alternative forms will be found on page 367 and following.*

### Eucharistic Prayer A

*The people remain standing. The Celebrant, whether bishop or priest, faces them and sings or says*

           The Lord be with you.
*People*     And also with you.
*Celebrant* Lift up your hearts.
*People*     We lift them to the Lord.
*Celebrant* Let us give thanks to the Lord our God.
*People*     It is right to give him thanks and praise.

*Then, facing the Holy Table, the Celebrant proceeds*

It is right, and a good and joyful thing, always and everywhere to give thanks to you, Father Almighty, Creator of heaven and earth.

*Here a Proper Preface is sung or said on all Sundays, and on other occasions as appointed.*

Therefore we praise you, joining our voices with Angels and Archangels and with all the company of heaven, who for ever sing this hymn to proclaim the glory of your Name:

*Celebrant and People*

Holy, holy, holy Lord, God of power and might,
heaven and earth are full of your glory.
    Hosanna in the highest.
Blessed is he who comes in the name of the Lord.
    Hosanna in the highest.

*The people stand or kneel.*

*Then the Celebrant continues*

Holy and gracious Father: In your infinite love you made us for yourself; and, when we had fallen into sin and become subject to evil and death, you, in your mercy, sent Jesus Christ, your only and eternal Son, to share our human nature, to live and die as one of us, to reconcile us to you, the God and Father of all.

He stretched out his arms upon the cross, and offered himself, in obedience to your will, a perfect sacrifice for the whole world.

*At the following words concerning the bread, the Celebrant is to hold it, or lay a hand upon it; and at the words concerning the cup, to hold or place a hand upon the cup and any other vessel containing wine to be consecrated.*

On the night he was handed over to suffering and death, our Lord Jesus Christ took bread; and when he had given thanks to you, he broke it, and gave it to his disciples, and said, "Take, eat: This is my Body, which is given for you. Do this for the remembrance of me."

After supper he took the cup of wine; and when he had given thanks, he gave it to them, and said, "Drink this, all of you: This is my Blood of the new Covenant, which is shed for you and for many for the forgiveness of sins. Whenever you drink it, do this for the remembrance of me."

Therefore we proclaim the mystery of faith:

*Celebrant and People*

Christ has died.
Christ is risen.
Christ will come again.

*The Celebrant continues*

We celebrate the memorial of our redemption, O Father, in this sacrifice of praise and thanksgiving. Recalling his death, resurrection, and ascension, we offer you these gifts.

Sanctify them by your Holy Spirit to be for your people the Body and Blood of your Son, the holy food and drink of new and unending life in him. Sanctify us also that we may faithfully receive this holy Sacrament, and serve you in unity, constancy, and peace; and at the last day bring us with all your saints into the joy of your eternal kingdom.

All this we ask through your Son Jesus Christ. By him, and with him, and in him, in the unity of the Holy Spirit all honor and glory is yours, Almighty Father, now and for ever. *AMEN.*

| | |
|---|---|
| And now, as our Savior Christ has taught us, we are bold to say, | As our Savior Christ has taught us, we now pray, |

*People and Celebrant*

| | |
|---|---|
| Our Father, who art in heaven,<br>   hallowed be thy Name,<br>   thy kingdom come,<br>   thy will be done,<br>      on earth as it is in heaven.<br>Give us this day our daily bread.<br>And forgive us our trespasses,<br>   as we forgive those<br>      who trespass against us.<br>And lead us not into temptation,<br>   but deliver us from evil.<br>For thine is the kingdom,<br>   and the power, and the glory,<br>   for ever and ever. Amen. | Our Father in heaven,<br>   hallowed be your Name,<br>   your kingdom come,<br>   your will be done,<br>      on earth as in heaven.<br>Give us today our daily bread.<br>Forgive us our sins<br>   as we forgive those<br>      who sin against us.<br>Save us from the time of trial,<br>   and deliver us from evil.<br>For the kingdom, the power,<br>   and the glory are yours,<br>   now and for ever. Amen. |

## The Breaking of the Bread

*The Celebrant breaks the consecrated Bread.*

*A period of silence is kept.*

*Then may be sung or said*

[Alleluia.] Christ our Passover is sacrificed for us;
*Therefore let us keep the feast.* [*Alleluia.*]

*In Lent, Alleluia is omitted, and may be omitted at other times except during Easter Season.*

*In place of, or in addition to, the preceding, some other suitable anthem may be used.*

*Facing the people, the Celebrant says the following Invitation*

The Gifts of God for the People of God.

*and may add*   Take them in remembrance that Christ died for
you, and feed on him in your hearts by faith,
with thanksgiving.

*The ministers receive the Sacrament in both kinds, and then immediately deliver it to the people.*

*The Bread and the Cup are given to the communicants with these words*

The Body (Blood) of our Lord Jesus Christ keep you in everlasting life. [*Amen.*]

*or with these words*

The Body of Christ, the bread of heaven. [*Amen.*]
The Blood of Christ, the cup of salvation. [*Amen.*]

*During the ministration of Communion, hymns, psalms, or anthems may be sung.*

*When necessary, the Celebrant consecrates additional bread and wine, using the form on page 408.*

*After Communion, the Celebrant says*

Let us pray.

*Celebrant and People*

Eternal God, heavenly Father,
you have graciously accepted us as living members
of your Son our Savior Jesus Christ,
and you have fed us with spiritual food
in the Sacrament of his Body and Blood.
Send us now into the world in peace,
and grant us strength and courage
to love and serve you
with gladness and singleness of heart;
through Christ our Lord. Amen.

*or the following*

*Holy Eucharist II*

Almighty and everliving God,
we thank you for feeding us with the spiritual food
of the most precious Body and Blood
of your Son our Savior Jesus Christ;
and for assuring us in these holy mysteries
that we are living members of the Body of your Son,
and heirs of your eternal kingdom.
And now, Father, send us out
to do the work you have given us to do,
to love and serve you
as faithful witnesses of Christ our Lord.
To him, to you, and to the Holy Spirit,
be honor and glory, now and for ever. Amen.

*The Bishop when present, or the Priest, may bless the people.*

*The Deacon, or the Celebrant, dismisses them with these words*

|  | Let us go forth in the name of Christ. |
|---|---|
| *People* | Thanks be to God. |

*or this*

| *Deacon* | Go in peace to love and serve the Lord. |
|---|---|
| *People* | Thanks be to God. |

*or this*

| *Deacon* | Let us go forth into the world, rejoicing in the power of the Spirit. |
|---|---|
| *People* | Thanks be to God. |

*or this*

| *Deacon* | Let us bless the Lord. |
|---|---|
| *People* | Thanks be to God. |

*From the Easter Vigil through the Day of Pentecost "Alleluia, alleluia" may be added to any of the dismissals.*

*The People respond*   Thanks be to God. Alleluia, alleluia.

# Alternative Forms of the Great Thanksgiving

## Eucharistic Prayer B

*The people remain standing. The Celebrant, whether bishop or priest, faces them and sings or says*

           The Lord be with you.
*People*     And also with you.
*Celebrant*  Lift up your hearts.
*People*     We lift them to the Lord.
*Celebrant*  Let us give thanks to the Lord our God.
*People*     It is right to give him thanks and praise.

*Then, facing the Holy Table, the Celebrant proceeds*

It is right, and a good and joyful thing, always and everywhere to give thanks to you, Father Almighty, Creator of heaven and earth.

*Here a Proper Preface is sung or said on all Sundays, and on other occasions as appointed.*

Therefore we praise you, joining our voices with Angels and Archangels and with all the company of heaven, who for ever sing this hymn to proclaim the glory of your Name:

*Celebrant and People*

Holy, holy, holy Lord, God of power and might,
heaven and earth are full of your glory.
    Hosanna in the highest.
Blessed is he who comes in the name of the Lord.
    Hosanna in the highest.

*The people stand or kneel.*

*Then the Celebrant continues*

We give thanks to you, O God, for the goodness and love which you have made known to us in creation; in the calling of Israel to be your people; in your Word spoken through the prophets; and above all in the Word made flesh, Jesus, your Son. For in these last days you sent him to be incarnate from the Virgin Mary, to be the Savior and Redeemer of the world. In him, you have delivered us from evil, and made us worthy to stand before you. In him, you have brought us out of error into truth, out of sin into righteousness, out of death into life.

*At the following words concerning the bread, the Celebrant is to hold it, or lay a hand upon it; and at the words concerning the cup, to hold or place a hand upon the cup and any other vessel containing wine to be consecrated.*

On the night before he died for us, our Lord Jesus Christ took bread; and when he had given thanks to you, he broke it, and gave it to his disciples, and said, "Take, eat: This is my Body, which is given for you. Do this for the remembrance of me."

After supper he took the cup of wine; and when he had given thanks, he gave it to them, and said, "Drink this, all of you: This is my Blood of the new Covenant, which is shed for you and for many for the forgiveness of sins. Whenever you drink it, do this for the remembrance of me."

Therefore, according to his command, O Father,

*Celebrant and People*

We remember his death,
We proclaim his resurrection,
We await his coming in glory;

*The Celebrant continues*

And we offer our sacrifice of praise and thanksgiving to you, O Lord of all; presenting to you, from your creation, this bread and this wine.

We pray you, gracious God, to send your Holy Spirit upon these gifts that they may be the Sacrament of the Body of Christ and his Blood of the new Covenant. Unite us to your Son in his sacrifice, that we may be acceptable through him, being sanctified by the Holy Spirit. In the fullness of time, put all things in subjection under your Christ, and bring us to that heavenly country where, with [_____ and] all your saints, we may enter the everlasting heritage of your sons and daughters; through Jesus Christ our Lord, the firstborn of all creation, the head of the Church, and the author of our salvation.

By him, and with him, and in him, in the unity of the Holy Spirit all honor and glory is yours, Almighty Father, now and for ever. AMEN.

| | |
|---|---|
| And now, as our Savior Christ has taught us, we are bold to say, | As our Savior Christ has taught us, we now pray, |

*Continue with the Lord's Prayer on page 364.*


## Eucharistic Prayer C

*In this prayer, the lines in italics are spoken by the People.*

*The Celebrant, whether bishop or priest, faces them and sings or says*

The Lord be with you.
*And also with you.*

Lift up your hearts.
*We lift them to the Lord.*

Let us give thanks to the Lord our God.
*It is right to give him thanks and praise.*

*Then, facing the Holy Table, the Celebrant proceeds*

God of all power, Ruler of the Universe, you are worthy of glory and praise.
*Glory to you for ever and ever.*

At your command all things came to be: the vast expanse of interstellar space, galaxies, suns, the planets in their courses, and this fragile earth, our island home.
*By your will they were created and have their being.*

From the primal elements you brought forth the human race, and blessed us with memory, reason, and skill. You made us the rulers of creation. But we turned against you, and betrayed your trust; and we turned against one another.
*Have mercy, Lord, for we are sinners in your sight.*

Again and again, you called us to return. Through prophets and sages you revealed your righteous Law. And in the fullness of time you sent your only Son, born of a woman, to fulfill your Law, to open for us the way of freedom and peace.
*By his blood, he reconciled us.*
*By his wounds, we are healed.*

And therefore we praise you, joining with the heavenly chorus, with prophets, apostles, and martyrs, and with all those in every generation who have looked to you in hope, to proclaim with them your glory, in their unending hymn:

*Celebrant and People*

Holy, holy, holy Lord, God of power and might,
heaven and earth are full of your glory.
    Hosanna in the highest.
Blessed is he who comes in the name of the Lord.
    Hosanna in the highest.

*The Celebrant continues*

And so, Father, we who have been redeemed by him, and made a new people by water and the Spirit, now bring before you these gifts. Sanctify them by your Holy Spirit to be the Body and Blood of Jesus Christ our Lord.

*At the following words concerning the bread, the Celebrant is to hold it, or lay a hand upon it; and at the words concerning the cup, to hold or place a hand upon the cup and any other vessel containing wine to be consecrated.*

On the night he was betrayed he took bread, said the blessing, broke the bread, and gave it to his friends, and said, "Take, eat: This is my Body, which is given for you. Do this for the remembrance of me."

After supper, he took the cup of wine, gave thanks, and said, "Drink this, all of you: This is my Blood of the new Covenant, which is shed for you and for many for the forgiveness of sins. Whenever you drink it, do this for the remembrance of me."

Remembering now his work of redemption, and offering to you this sacrifice of thanksgiving,
*We celebrate his death and resurrection,*
*as we await the day of his coming.*

Lord God of our Fathers; God of Abraham, Isaac, and
Jacob; God and Father of our Lord Jesus Christ: Open our
eyes to see your hand at work in the world about us. Deliver
us from the presumption of coming to this Table for solace
only, and not for strength; for pardon only, and not for
renewal. Let the grace of this Holy Communion make us one
body, one spirit in Christ, that we may worthily serve the
world in his name.
*Risen Lord, be known to us in the breaking of the Bread.*

Accept these prayers and praises, Father, through Jesus
Christ our great High Priest, to whom, with you and the
Holy Spirit, your Church gives honor, glory, and worship,
from generation to generation. AMEN.

| And now, as our Savior | As our Savior Christ |
| Christ has taught us, | has taught us, |
| we are bold to say, | we now pray, |

*Continue with the Lord's Prayer on page 364.*


### Eucharistic Prayer D

*The people remain standing. The Celebrant, whether bishop or priest, faces them and sings or says*

          The Lord be with you.
*People*    And also with you.
*Celebrant*  Lift up your hearts.
*People*    We lift them to the Lord.
*Celebrant*  Let us give thanks to the Lord our God.
*People*    It is right to give him thanks and praise.

*Then, facing the Holy Table, the Celebrant proceeds*

It is truly right to glorify you, Father, and to give you thanks; for you alone are God, living and true, dwelling in light inaccessible from before time and for ever.

Fountain of life and source of all goodness, you made all things and fill them with your blessing; you created them to rejoice in the splendor of your radiance.

Countless throngs of angels stand before you to serve you night and day; and, beholding the glory of your presence, they offer you unceasing praise. Joining with them, and giving voice to every creature under heaven, we acclaim you, and glorify your Name, as we sing (say),

*Celebrant and People*

Holy, holy, holy Lord, God of power and might,
heaven and earth are full of your glory.
    Hosanna in the highest.
Blessed is he who comes in the name of the Lord.
    Hosanna in the highest.

*The people stand or kneel.*

*Then the Celebrant continues*

We acclaim you, holy Lord, glorious in power. Your mighty works reveal your wisdom and love. You formed us in your own image, giving the whole world into our care, so that, in obedience to you, our Creator, we might rule and serve all your creatures. When our disobedience took us far from you, you did not abandon us to the power of death. In your mercy you came to our help, so that in seeking you we might find you. Again and again you called us into covenant with you, and through the prophets you taught us to hope for salvation.

Father, you loved the world so much that in the fullness of time you sent your only Son to be our Savior. Incarnate by the Holy Spirit, born of the Virgin Mary, he lived as one of us, yet without sin. To the poor he proclaimed the good news of salvation; to prisoners, freedom; to the sorrowful, joy. To fulfill your purpose he gave himself up to death; and, rising from the grave, destroyed death, and made the whole creation new.

And, that we might live no longer for ourselves, but for him who died and rose for us, he sent the Holy Spirit, his own first gift for those who believe, to complete his work in the world, and to bring to fulfillment the sanctification of all.

*At the following words concerning the bread, the Celebrant is to hold it, or lay a hand upon it; and at the words concerning the cup, to hold or place a hand upon the cup and any other vessel containing wine to be consecrated.*

When the hour had come for him to be glorified by you, his heavenly Father, having loved his own who were in the world, he loved them to the end; at supper with them he took bread, and when he had given thanks to you, he broke it, and gave it to his disciples, and said,"Take, eat: This is my Body, which is given for you. Do this for the remembrance of me."

After supper he took the cup of wine; and when he had given thanks, he gave it to them, and said,"Drink this, all of you: This is my Blood of the new Covenant, which is shed for you and for many for the forgiveness of sins. Whenever you drink it, do this for the remembrance of me."

Father, we now celebrate this memorial of our redemption. Recalling Christ's death and his descent among the dead, proclaiming his resurrection and ascension to your right hand, awaiting his coming in glory; and offering to you, from the gifts you have given us, this bread and this cup, we praise you and we bless you.

*Celebrant and People*

We praise you, we bless you,
we give thanks to you,
and we pray to you, Lord our God.

*The Celebrant continues*

Lord, we pray that in your goodness and mercy your Holy Spirit may descend upon us, and upon these gifts, sanctifying them and showing them to be holy gifts for your holy people, the bread of life and the cup of salvation, the Body and Blood of your Son Jesus Christ.

Grant that all who share this bread and cup may become one body and one spirit, a living sacrifice in Christ, to the praise of your Name.

Remember, Lord, your one holy catholic and apostolic Church, redeemed by the blood of your Christ. Reveal its unity, guard its faith, and preserve it in peace.

[Remember (*NN*. and) all who minister in your Church.]
[Remember all your people, and those who seek your truth.]
[Remember _____.]
[Remember all who have died in the peace of Christ, and those whose faith is known to you alone; bring them into the place of eternal joy and light.]

And grant that we may find our inheritance with [the Blessed Virgin Mary, with patriarchs, prophets, apostles, and martyrs, (with_____) and] all the saints who have found favor with you in ages past. We praise you in union with them and give you glory through your Son Jesus Christ our Lord.

Through Christ, and with Christ, and in Christ, all honor and glory are yours, Almighty God and Father, in the unity of the Holy Spirit, for ever and ever. *AMEN.*

| | |
|---|---|
| And now, as our Savior Christ has taught us, we are bold to say, | As our Savior Christ has taught us, we now pray, |

*Continue with the Lord's Prayer on page 364.*

## Offertory Sentences

*One of the following, or some other appropriate sentence of Scripture, may be used*

Offer to God a sacrifice of thanksgiving, and make good your vows to the Most High.   *Psalm 50:14*

Ascribe to the Lord the honor due his Name; bring offerings and come into his courts.   *Psalm 96:8*

Walk in love, as Christ loved us and gave himself for us, an offering and sacrifice to God.   *Ephesians 5:2*

I appeal to you, brethren, by the mercies of God, to present yourselves as a living sacrifice, holy and acceptable to God, which is your spiritual worship.   *Romans 12:1*

If you are offering your gift at the altar, and there remember that your brother has something against you, leave your gift there before the altar and go; first be reconciled to your brother, and then come and offer your gift.   *Matthew 5:23, 24*

Through Christ let us continually offer to God the sacrifice of praise, that is, the fruit of lips that acknowledge his Name.

But do not neglect to do good and to share what you have, for such sacrifices are pleasing to God.  *Hebrews 13:15,16*

O Lord our God, you are worthy to receive glory and honor and power; because you have created all things, and by your will they were created and have their being.  *Revelation 4:11*

Yours, O Lord, is the greatness, the power, the glory, the victory, and the majesty. For everything in heaven and on earth is yours. Yours, O Lord, is the kingdom, and you are exalted as head over all.  *1 Chronicles 29:11*

*or this bidding*

Let us with gladness present the offerings and oblations of our life and labor to the Lord.

# Proper Prefaces

### Preface of the Lord's Day

*To be used on Sundays as appointed, but not on the succeeding weekdays*

1. Of God the Father

For you are the source of light and life; you made us in your image, and called us to new life in Jesus Christ our Lord.

*or this*

2. Of God the Son

Through Jesus Christ our Lord; who on the first day of the week overcame death and the grave, and by his glorious resurrection opened to us the way of everlasting life.

*or the following*

### 3. Of God the Holy Spirit

For by water and the Holy Spirit you have made us a new people in Jesus Christ our Lord, to show forth your glory in all the world.

## Prefaces for Seasons

*To be used on Sundays and weekdays alike, except as otherwise appointed for Holy Days and Various Occasions*

### Advent

Because you sent your beloved Son to redeem us from sin and death, and to make us heirs in him of everlasting life; that when he shall come again in power and great triumph to judge the world, we may without shame or fear rejoice to behold his appearing.

### Incarnation

Because you gave Jesus Christ, your only Son, to be born for us; who, by the mighty power of the Holy Spirit, was made perfect Man of the flesh of the Virgin Mary his mother; so that we might be delivered from the bondage of sin, and receive power to become your children.

### Epiphany

Because in the mystery of the Word made flesh, you have caused a new light to shine in our hearts, to give the knowledge of your glory in the face of your Son Jesus Christ our Lord.

*Lent*

Through Jesus Christ our Lord, who was tempted in every way as we are, yet did not sin. By his grace we are able to triumph over every evil, and to live no longer for ourselves alone, but for him who died for us and rose again.

*or this*

You bid your faithful people cleanse their hearts, and prepare with joy for the Paschal feast; that, fervent in prayer and in works of mercy, and renewed by your Word and Sacraments, they may come to the fullness of grace which you have prepared for those who love you.

*Holy Week*

Through Jesus Christ our Lord. For our sins he was lifted high upon the cross, that he might draw the whole world to himself; and, by his suffering and death, he became the source of eternal salvation for all who put their trust in him.

*Easter*

But chiefly are we bound to praise you for the glorious resurrection of your Son Jesus Christ our Lord; for he is the true Paschal Lamb, who was sacrificed for us, and has taken away the sin of the world. By his death he has destroyed death, and by his rising to life again he has won for us everlasting life.

*Ascension*

Through your dearly beloved Son Jesus Christ our Lord. After his glorious resurrection he openly appeared to his disciples, and in their sight ascended into heaven, to prepare a place for us; that where he is, there we might also be, and reign with him in glory.

*Pentecost*

Through Jesus Christ our Lord. In fulfillment of his true promise, the Holy Spirit came down [on this day] from heaven, lighting upon the disciples, to teach them and to lead them into all truth; uniting peoples of many tongues in the confession of one faith, and giving to your Church the power to serve you as a royal priesthood, and to preach the Gospel to all nations.

**Prefaces for Other Occasions**

*Trinity Sunday*

For with your co-eternal Son and Holy Spirit, you are one God, one Lord, in Trinity of Persons and in Unity of Being: and we celebrate the one and equal glory of you, O Father, and of the Son, and of the Holy Spirit.

*All Saints*

For in the multitude of your saints, you have surrounded us with a great cloud of witnesses, that we might rejoice in their fellowship, and run with endurance the race that is set before us; and, together with them, receive the crown of glory that never fades away.

*A Saint*

For the wonderful grace and virtue declared in all your saints, who have been the chosen vessels of your grace, and the lights of the world in their generations.

*or this*

Because in the obedience of your saints you have given us an example of righteousness, and in their eternal joy a glorious pledge of the hope of our calling.

*or this*

Because you are greatly glorified in the assembly of your saints. All your creatures praise you, and your faithful servants bless you, confessing before the rulers of this world the great Name of your only Son.

*Apostles and Ordinations*

Through the great shepherd of your flock, Jesus Christ our Lord; who after his resurrection sent forth his apostles to preach the Gospel and to teach all nations; and promised to be with them always, even to the end of the ages.

*Dedication of a Church*

Through Jesus Christ our great High Priest, in whom we are built up as living stones of a holy temple, that we might offer before you a sacrifice of praise and prayer which is holy and pleasing in your sight.

*Baptism*

Because in Jesus Christ our Lord you have received us as your sons and daughters, made us citizens of your kingdom, and given us the Holy Spirit to guide us into all truth.

*Marriage*

Because in the love of wife and husband, you have given us an image of the heavenly Jerusalem, adorned as a bride for her bridegroom, your Son Jesus Christ our Lord; who loves her and gave himself for her, that he might make the whole creation new.

*Commemoration of the Dead*

Through Jesus Christ our Lord; who rose victorious from the dead, and comforts us with the blessed hope of everlasting life. For to your faithful people, O Lord, life is changed, not ended; and when our mortal body lies in death, there is prepared for us a dwelling place eternal in the heavens.

# The Prayers of the People

Prayer is offered with intercession for

The Universal Church, its members, and its mission
The Nation and all in authority
The welfare of the world
The concerns of the local community
Those who suffer and those in any trouble
The departed (with commemoration of a saint when appropriate)

*Any of the forms which follow may be used.*

*Adaptations or insertions suitable to the occasion may be made.*

*Any of the forms may be conformed to the language of the Rite being used.*

*A bar in the margin indicates petitions which may be omitted.*

*The Celebrant may introduce the Prayers with a sentence of invitation related to the occasion, or the season, or the Proper of the Day.*

## Form I

*Deacon or other leader*

With all our heart and with all our mind, let us pray to the Lord, saying, "Lord, have mercy."

For the peace from above, for the loving kindness of God, and for the salvation of our souls, let us pray to the Lord.
*Lord, have mercy.*

For the peace of the world, for the welfare of the holy Church of God, and for the unity of all peoples, let us pray to the Lord.
*Lord, have mercy.*

For our Bishop, and for all the clergy and people, let us pray to the Lord.
*Lord, have mercy.*

For our President, for the leaders of the nations, and for all in authority, let us pray to the Lord.
*Lord, have mercy.*

For this city (town, village, _____ ), for every city and community, and for those who live in them, let us pray to the Lord.
*Lord, have mercy.*

For seasonable weather, and for an abundance of the fruits of the earth, let us pray to the Lord.
*Lord, have mercy.*

For the good earth which God has given us, and for the wisdom and will to conserve it, let us pray to the Lord.
*Lord, have mercy.*

For those who travel on land, on water, or in the air [or through outer space], let us pray to the Lord.
*Lord, have mercy.*

For the aged and infirm, for the widowed and orphans, and for the sick and the suffering, let us pray to the Lord.
*Lord, have mercy.*

For _____ , let us pray to the Lord.
*Lord, have mercy.*

For the poor and the oppressed, for the unemployed and the destitute, for prisoners and captives, and for all who remember and care for them, let us pray to the Lord.
*Lord, have mercy.*

For all who have died in the hope of the resurrection, and for all the departed, let us pray to the Lord.
*Lord, have mercy.*

For deliverance from all danger, violence, oppression, and degradation, let us pray to the Lord.
*Lord, have mercy.*

For the absolution and remission of our sins and offenses, let us pray to the Lord.
*Lord, have mercy.*

That we may end our lives in faith and hope, without suffering and without reproach, let us pray to the Lord.
*Lord, have mercy.*

Defend us, deliver us, and in thy compassion protect us, O Lord, by thy grace.
*Lord, have mercy.*

In the communion of [_____ and of all the] saints, let us commend ourselves, and one another, and all our life, to Christ our God.
*To thee, O Lord our God.*

*Silence*

*The Celebrant adds a concluding Collect.*

## Form II

*In the course of the silence after each bidding, the People offer their own prayers, either silently or aloud.*

I ask your prayers for God's people throughout the world; for our Bishop(s) _____ ; for this gathering; and for all ministers and people.
Pray for the Church.

*Silence*

I ask your prayers for peace; for goodwill among nations; and for the well-being of all people.
Pray for justice and peace.

*Silence*

I ask your prayers for the poor, the sick, the hungry, the oppressed, and those in prison.
Pray for those in any need or trouble.

*Silence*

I ask your prayers for all who seek God, or a deeper knowledge of him.
Pray that they may find and be found by him.

*Silence*

I ask your prayers for the departed [especially _____ ].
Pray for those who have died.

*Silence*

*Members of the congregation may ask the prayers or the thanksgivings of those present*

I ask your prayers for _____ .

I ask your thanksgiving for _____ .

*Silence*

Praise God for those in every generation in whom Christ has been honored [especially _____ whom we remember today].
Pray that we may have grace to glorify Christ in our own day.

*Silence*

*The Celebrant adds a concluding Collect.*

## Form III

*The Leader and People pray responsively*

Father, we pray for your holy Catholic Church;
*That we all may be one.*

Grant that every member of the Church may truly and humbly serve you;
*That your Name may be glorified by all people.*

We pray for all bishops, priests, and deacons;
*That they may be faithful ministers of your Word and Sacraments.*

We pray for all who govern and hold authority in the nations of the world;
*That there may be justice and peace on the earth.*

Give us grace to do your will in all that we undertake;
*That our works may find favor in your sight.*

Have compassion on those who suffer from any grief or trouble;
*That they may be delivered from their distress.*

Give to the departed eternal rest;
*Let light perpetual shine upon them.*

We praise you for your saints who have entered into joy;
*May we also come to share in your heavenly kingdom.*

Let us pray for our own needs and those of others.

*Silence*

*The People may add their own petitions.*

*The Celebrant adds a concluding Collect.*

## Form IV

*Deacon or other leader*

Let us pray for the Church and for the world.

Grant, Almighty God, that all who confess your Name may be united in your truth, live together in your love, and reveal your glory in the world.

*Silence*

Lord, in your mercy
*Hear our prayer.*

Guide the people of this land, and of all the nations, in the ways of justice and peace; that we may honor one another and serve the common good.

*Silence*

Lord, in your mercy
*Hear our prayer.*

Give us all a reverence for the earth as your own creation, that we may use its resources rightly in the service of others and to your honor and glory.

*Silence*

Lord, in your mercy
*Hear our prayer.*

Bless all whose lives are closely linked with ours, and grant that we may serve Christ in them, and love one another as he loves us.

*Silence*

Lord, in your mercy
*Hear our prayer.*

Comfort and heal all those who suffer in body, mind, or spirit; give them courage and hope in their troubles, and bring them the joy of your salvation.

*Silence*

Lord, in your mercy
*Hear our prayer.*

We commend to your mercy all who have died, that your will for them may be fulfilled; and we pray that we may share with all your saints in your eternal kingdom.

*Silence*

Lord, in your mercy
*Hear our prayer.*

*The Celebrant adds a concluding Collect.*

**Form V**

*Deacon or other leader*

In peace, let us pray to the Lord, saying, "Lord, have mercy" (*or* "Kyrie eleison").

For the holy Church of God, that it may be filled with truth and love, and be found without fault at the day of your coming, we pray to you, O Lord.

*Here and after every petition the People respond*

*Kyrie eleison.*   or   *Lord, have mercy.*

For N. our Presiding Bishop, for N. (N.) our own bishop(s), for all bishops and other ministers, and for all the holy people of God, we pray to you, O Lord.

For all who fear God and believe in you, Lord Christ, that our divisions may cease, and that all may be one as you and the Father are one, we pray to you, O Lord.

For the mission of the Church, that in faithful witness it may preach the Gospel to the ends of the earth, we pray to you, O Lord.

For those who do not yet believe, and for those who have lost their faith, that they may receive the light of the Gospel, we pray to you, O Lord.

For the peace of the world, that a spirit of respect and forbearance may grow among nations and peoples, we pray to you, O Lord.

For those in positions of public trust [especially _____ ], that they may serve justice, and promote the dignity and freedom of every person, we pray to you, O Lord.

For all who live and work in this community [especially _____ ], we pray to you, O Lord.

For a blessing upon all human labor, and for the right use of the riches of creation, that the world may be freed from poverty, famine, and disaster, we pray to you, O Lord.

For the poor, the persecuted, the sick, and all who suffer; for refugees, prisoners, and all who are in danger; that they may be relieved and protected, we pray to you, O Lord.

For this *congregation* [for those who are present, and for those who are absent], that we may be delivered from hardness of heart, and show forth your glory in all that we do, we pray to you, O Lord.

For our enemies and those who wish us harm; and for all whom we have injured or offended, we pray to you, O Lord.

For ourselves; for the forgiveness of our sins, and for the grace of the Holy Spirit to amend our lives, we pray to you, O Lord.

For all who have commended themselves to our prayers; for our families, friends, and neighbors; that being freed from anxiety, they may live in joy, peace, and health, we pray to you, O Lord.

For _____ , we pray to you, O Lord.

For all who have died in the communion of your Church, and those whose faith is known to you alone, that, with all the saints, they may have rest in that place where there is no pain or grief, but life eternal, we pray to you, O Lord.

Rejoicing in the fellowship of [the ever-blessed Virgin Mary, (*blessed N.*) and] all the saints, let us commend ourselves, and one another, and all our life to Christ our God.
*To you, O Lord our God.*

*Silence*

*The Celebrant adds a concluding Collect, or the following Doxology*

For yours is the majesty, O Father, Son, and Holy Spirit; yours is the kingdom and the power and the glory, now and for ever. *Amen.*

**Form VI**

*The Leader and People pray responsively*

In peace, we pray to you, Lord God.

*Silence*

For all people in their daily life and work;
*For our families, friends, and neighbors, and for those who are alone.*

For this community, the nation, and the world;
*For all who work for justice, freedom, and peace.*

For the just and proper use of your creation;
*For the victims of hunger, fear, injustice, and oppression.*

For all who are in danger, sorrow, or any kind of trouble;
*For those who minister to the sick, the friendless, and the needy.*

For the peace and unity of the Church of God;
*For all who proclaim the Gospel, and all who seek the Truth.*

For [N. our Presiding Bishop, and N. (N.) our Bishop(s); and for] all bishops and other ministers;
*For all who serve God in his Church.*

For the special needs and concerns of this congregation.

*Silence*

*The People may add their own petitions*

Hear us, Lord;
*For your mercy is great.*

We thank you, Lord, for all the blessings of this life.

*Silence*

*The People may add their own thanksgivings*

We will exalt you, O God our King;
*And praise your Name for ever and ever.*

We pray for all who have died, that they may have a place in your eternal kingdom.

*Silence*

*The People may add their own petitions*

Lord, let your loving-kindness be upon them;
*Who put their trust in you.*

We pray to you also for the forgiveness of our sins.

*Silence may be kept.*

*Leader and People*

Have mercy upon us, most merciful Father;
in your compassion forgive us our sins,
known and unknown,
things done and left undone;
and so uphold us by your Spirit
that we may live and serve you in newness of life,
to the honor and glory of your Name;
through Jesus Christ our Lord. Amen.

*The Celebrant concludes with an absolution or a suitable Collect.*

# The Collect at the Prayers

For the concluding Collect, the Celebrant selects

(a) a Collect appropriate to the Season or occasion being celebrated;

(b) a Collect expressive of some special need in the life of the local congregation;

(c) a Collect for the mission of the Church;

(d) a general Collect such as the following:

**1**

Lord, hear the prayers of *thy* people; and what we have asked faithfully, grant that we may obtain effectually, to the glory of *thy* Name; through Jesus Christ our Lord. *Amen.*

**2**

Heavenly Father, you have promised to hear what we ask in the Name of your Son: Accept and fulfill our petitions, we pray, not as we ask in our ignorance, nor as we deserve in our sinfulness, but as you know and love us in your Son Jesus Christ our Lord. *Amen.*

**3**

Almighty and eternal God, ruler of all things in heaven and earth: Mercifully accept the prayers of your people, and strengthen us to do your will; through Jesus Christ our Lord. *Amen.*

**4**

Almighty God, to whom our needs are known before we ask, help us to ask only what accords with your will; and those good things which we dare not, or in our blindness cannot ask, grant us for the sake of your Son Jesus Christ our Lord. *Amen.*

5

O Lord our God, accept the fervent prayers of your people; in the multitude of your mercies, look with compassion upon us and all who turn to you for help; for you are gracious, O lover of souls, and to you we give glory, Father, Son, and Holy Spirit, now and for ever. *Amen.*

6

Lord Jesus Christ, you said to your apostles, "Peace I give to you; my own peace I leave with you:" Regard not our sins, but the faith of your Church, and give to us the peace and unity of that heavenly City, where with the Father and the Holy Spirit, you live and reign, now and for ever. *Amen.*

7

Hasten, O Father, the coming of *thy* kingdom; and grant that we *thy* servants, who now live by faith, may with joy behold *thy* Son at his coming in glorious majesty; even Jesus Christ, our only Mediator and Advocate. *Amen.*

8

Almighty God, by your Holy Spirit you have made us one with your saints in heaven and on earth: Grant that in our earthly pilgrimage we may always be supported by this fellowship of love and prayer, and know ourselves to be surrounded by their witness to your power and mercy. We ask this for the sake of Jesus Christ, in whom all our intercessions are acceptable through the Spirit, and who lives and reigns for ever and ever. *Amen.*

# Communion under Special Circumstances

*This form is intended for use with those who for reasonable cause cannot be present at a public celebration of the Eucharist.*

*When persons are unable to be present for extended periods, it is desirable that the priest arrange to celebrate the Eucharist with them from time to time on a regular basis, using either the Proper of the Day or one of those appointed for Various Occasions. If it is necessary to shorten the service, the priest may begin the celebration at the Offertory, but it is desirable that a passage from the Gospel first be read.*

*At other times, or when desired, such persons may be communicated from the reserved Sacrament, using the following form.*

*It is desirable that fellow parishioners, relatives, and friends be present, when possible, to communicate with them.*

*The Celebrant, whether priest or deacon, reads a passage of Scripture appropriate to the day or occasion, or else one of the following*

God so loved the world that he gave his only Son, that whoever believes in him should not perish, but have eternal life. . *John 3:16*

Jesus said,"I am the bread of life; whoever comes to me shall not hunger, and whoever believes in me shall never thirst." *John 6:35*

Jesus said, "I am the living bread which came down from heaven; if anyone eats of this bread, he will live for ever; and the bread which I shall give for the life of the world is my flesh. For my flesh is food indeed, and my blood is drink indeed. Whoever eats my flesh and drinks my blood abides in me, and I in him." *John 6:51,55-56*

Jesus said, "Abide in me, as I in you. As the branch cannot bear fruit by itself, unless it abides in the vine, neither can you, unless you abide in me. I am the vine, you are the branches. By this my Father is glorified, that you bear much fruit, and so prove to be my disciples. As the Father has loved me, so have I loved you; abide in my love." *John 15:4-5a,8-9*

*After the Reading, the Celebrant may comment on it briefly.*

*Suitable prayers may be offered, concluding with the following or some other Collect*

Almighty Father, whose dear Son, on the night before he suffered, instituted the Sacrament of his Body and Blood: Mercifully grant that we may receive it thankfully in remembrance of Jesus Christ our Lord, who in these holy mysteries gives us a pledge of eternal life; and who lives and reigns for ever and ever. *Amen.*

*A Confession of Sin may follow. The following or some other form is used*

Most merciful God,
we confess that we have sinned against you
in thought, word, and deed,
by what we have done,
and by what we have left undone.
We have not loved you with our whole heart;
we have not loved our neighbors as ourselves.

We are truly sorry and we humbly repent.
For the sake of your Son Jesus Christ,
have mercy on us and forgive us;
that we may delight in your will,
and walk in your ways,
to the glory of your Name. Amen.

*The Priest alone says*

Almighty God have mercy on you, forgive you all your sins through our Lord Jesus Christ, strengthen you in all goodness, and by the power of the Holy Spirit keep you in eternal life. *Amen.*

*A deacon using the preceding form substitutes "us" for "you" and "our" for "your."*

*The Peace may then be exchanged.*

*The Lord's Prayer is said, the Celebrant first saying*

Let us pray in the words our Savior Christ has taught us.

| | |
|---|---|
| Our Father, who art in heaven,<br>   hallowed be thy Name,<br>   thy kingdom come,<br>   thy will be done,<br>      on earth as it is in heaven.<br>Give us this day our daily bread.<br>And forgive us our trespasses,<br>   as we forgive those<br>      who trespass against us.<br>And lead us not into temptation,<br>   but deliver us from evil.<br>For thine is the kingdom,<br>   and the power, and the glory,<br>      for ever and ever. Amen. | Our Father in heaven,<br>   hallowed be your Name,<br>   your kingdom come,<br>   your will be done,<br>      on earth as in heaven.<br>Give us today our daily bread.<br>Forgive us our sins<br>   as we forgive those<br>      who sin against us.<br>Save us from the time of trial,<br>   and deliver us from evil.<br>For the kingdom, the power,<br>   and the glory are yours,<br>      now and for ever. Amen. |

*The Celebrant may say the following Invitation*

The Gifts of God for the People of God.

*and may add*   Take them in remembrance that Christ died for you, and feed on him in your hearts by faith, with thanksgiving.

*The Sacrament is administered with the following or other words*

The Body (Blood) of our Lord Jesus Christ keep you in everlasting life. [*Amen.*]

*One of the usual postcommunion prayers is then said, or the following*

Gracious Father, we give you praise and thanks for this Holy Communion of the Body and Blood of your beloved Son Jesus Christ, the pledge of our redemption; and we pray that it may bring us forgiveness of our sins, strength in our weakness, and everlasting salvation; through Jesus Christ our Lord. Amen.

*The service concludes with a blessing or with a dismissal*

Let us bless the Lord.
*Thanks be to God.*

# An Order for Celebrating the Holy Eucharist

*This rite requires careful preparation by the Priest and other participants.*

*It is not intended for use at the principal Sunday or weekly celebration of the Holy Eucharist.*

## The People and Priest

**Gather in the Lord's Name**

**Proclaim and Respond to the Word of God**

The proclamation and response may include readings, song, talk, dance, instrumental music, other art forms, silence. A reading from the Gospel is always included.

**Pray for the World and the Church**

## Exchange the Peace

Either here or elsewhere in the service, all greet one another in the name of the Lord.

## Prepare the Table

Some of those present prepare the table; the bread, the cup of wine, and other offerings, are placed upon it.

## Make Eucharist

The Great Thanksgiving is said by the Priest in the name of the gathering, using one of the eucharistic prayers provided.

The people respond—Amen!

## Break the Bread

## Share the Gifts of God

The Body and Blood of the Lord are shared in a reverent manner; after all have received, any of the Sacrament that remains is then consumed.

*When a common meal or Agapé is a part of the celebration, it follows here.*

# At the Great Thanksgiving

*In making Eucharist, the Celebrant uses one of the Eucharistic Prayers from Rite One or Rite Two, or one of the following forms*

## Form 1

*Celebrant*  The Lord be with you.
*People*  And also with you.
*Celebrant*  Lift up your hearts.
*People*  We lift them to the Lord.
*Celebrant*  Let us give thanks to the Lord our God.
*People*  It is right to give him thanks and praise.

*The Celebrant gives thanks to God the Father for his work in creation and his revelation of himself to his people;*

*Recalls before God, when appropriate, the particular occasion being celebrated;*

*Incorporates or adapts the Proper Preface of the day, if desired.*

*If the Sanctus is to be included, it is introduced with these or similar words*

And so we join the saints and angels in proclaiming your glory, as we sing (say),

*Celebrant and People*

Holy, holy, holy Lord, God of power and might,
heaven and earth are full of your glory.
    Hosanna in the highest.
Blessed is he who comes in the name of the Lord.
    Hosanna in the highest.

*The Celebrant now praises God for the salvation of the world through Jesus Christ our Lord.*

*The Prayer continues with these words*

And so, Father, we bring you these gifts. Sanctify them by your Holy Spirit to be for your people the Body and Blood of Jesus Christ our Lord.

*At the following words concerning the bread, the Celebrant is to hold it, or lay a hand upon it; and at the words concerning the cup, to hold or place a hand upon the cup and any other vessel containing wine to be consecrated.*

On the night he was betrayed he took bread, said the blessing, broke the bread, and gave it to his friends, and said, "Take, eat: This is my Body, which is given for you. Do this for the remembrance of me."

After supper, he took the cup of wine, gave thanks, and said, "Drink this, all of you. This is my Blood of the new Covenant, which is shed for you and for many for the forgiveness of sins. Whenever you drink it, do this for the remembrance of me."

Father, we now celebrate the memorial of your Son. By means of this holy bread and cup, we show forth the sacrifice of his death, and proclaim his resurrection, until he comes again.

Gather us by this Holy Communion into one body in your Son Jesus Christ. Make us a living sacrifice of praise.

By him, and with him, and in him, in the unity of the Holy Spirit all honor and glory is yours, Almighty Father, now and for ever. AMEN.

## Form 2

*Celebrant*   The grace of our Lord Jesus Christ and the love of God and the fellowship of the Holy Spirit be with you all.
*People*   And also with you.
*Celebrant*   Lift up your hearts.
*People*   We lift them to the Lord.
*Celebrant*   Let us give thanks to the Lord our God.
*People*   It is right to give him thanks and praise.

*The Celebrant gives thanks to God the Father for his work in creation and his revelation of himself to his people;*

*Recalls before God, when appropriate, the particular occasion being celebrated;*

*Incorporates or adapts the Proper Preface of the day, if desired.*

*If the Sanctus is to be included, it is introduced with these or similar words*

And so we join the saints and angels in proclaiming your glory, and we sing (say),

*Celebrant and People*

Holy, holy, holy Lord, God of power and might,
heaven and earth are full of your glory.
    Hosanna in the highest.
Blessed is he who comes in the name of the Lord.
    Hosanna in the highest.

*The Celebrant now praises God for the salvation of the world through Jesus Christ our Lord.*

*At the following words concerning the bread, the Celebrant is to hold it, or lay a hand upon it; and at the words concerning the cup, to hold or place a hand upon the cup and any other vessel containing wine to be consecrated.*

On the night he was handed over to suffering and death, our Lord Jesus Christ took bread; and when he had given thanks to you, he broke it, and gave it to his disciples, and said, "Take, eat: This is my Body, which is given for you. Do this for the remembrance of me."

After supper he took the cup of wine; and when he had given thanks, he gave it to them, and said, "Drink this, all of you: This is my Blood of the new Covenant, which is shed for you and for many for the forgiveness of sins. Whenever you drink it, do this for the remembrance of me."

Recalling now his suffering and death, and celebrating his resurrection and ascension, we await his coming in glory.

Accept, O Lord, our sacrifice of praise, this memorial of our redemption.

Send your Holy Spirit upon these gifts. Let them be for us the Body and Blood of your Son. And grant that we who eat this bread and drink this cup may be filled with your life and goodness.

*The Celebrant then prays that all may receive the benefits of Christ's work, and the renewal of the Holy Spirit.*

*The Prayer concludes with these or similar words*

All this we ask through your Son Jesus Christ. By him, and with him, and in him, in the unity of the Holy Spirit all honor and glory is yours, Almighty Father, now and for ever. AMEN.

# Additional Directions

The Holy Table is spread with a clean white cloth during the celebration.

When the Great Litany is sung or said immediately before the Eucharist, the Litany concludes with the Kyries, and the Eucharist begins with the Salutation and the Collect of the Day. The Prayers of the People following the Creed may be omitted.

When a psalm is used, it may be concluded with Gloria Patri. In Rite One services, the following form of the Gloria may be used:

Glory be to the Father, and to the Son, *
 and to the Holy Ghost:

As it was in the beginning, is now, and ever shall be, *
 world without end. Amen.

The Kyrie eleison (or "Lord, have mercy") may be sung or said in threefold, sixfold, or ninefold form. The Trisagion, "Holy God," may be sung or said three times, or antiphonally.

Gloria in excelsis, or the hymn used in place of it, is sung or said from Christmas Day through the Feast of the Epiphany; on Sundays from Easter Day through the Day of Pentecost, on all the days of Easter Week, and on Ascension Day; and at other times as desired; but it is not used on the Sundays or ordinary weekdays of Advent or Lent.

It is desirable that the Lessons be read from a lectern or pulpit, and that the Gospel be read from the same lectern, or from the pulpit, or from the midst of the congregation. It is desirable that the Lessons and Gospel be read from a book or books of appropriate size and dignity.

When a portion of the congregation is composed of persons whose native tongue is other than English, a reader appointed by the celebrant may read the Gospel in the language of the people, either in place of, or in addition to, the Gospel in English.

If there is no Communion, all that is appointed through the Prayers of the People may be said. (If it is desired to include a Confession of Sin, the service begins with the Penitential Order.) A hymn or anthem may then be sung, and the offerings of the people received. The service may then conclude with the Lord's Prayer; and with either the Grace or a blessing, or with the exchange of the Peace.

In the absence of a priest, all that is described above, except for the blessing, may be said by a deacon, or, if there is no deacon, by a lay reader.

The greeting, "The peace of the Lord be always with you," is addressed to the entire assembly. In the exchange between individuals which may follow, any appropriate words of greeting may be used. If preferred, the exchange of the Peace may take place at the time of the administration of the Sacrament (before or after the sentence of Invitation).

Necessary announcements may be made before the service, after the Creed, before the Offertory, or at the end of the service, as convenient.

It is the function of a deacon to make ready the Table for the celebration, preparing and placing upon it the bread and cup of wine. It is customary to add a little water to the wine. The deacon may be assisted by other ministers.

During the Great Thanksgiving, it is appropriate that there be only one chalice on the Altar, and, if need be, a flagon of wine from which additional chalices may be filled after the Breaking of the Bread.

The following anthem may be used at the Breaking of the Bread:

Lamb of God, you take away the sins of the world:
    have mercy on us.
Lamb of God, you take away the sins of the world:
    have mercy on us.
Lamb of God, you take away the sins of the world:
    grant us peace.

While the people are coming forward to receive Communion, the celebrant receives the Sacrament in both kinds. The bishops, priests, and deacons at the Holy Table then communicate, and after them the people.

Opportunity is always to be given to every communicant to receive the consecrated Bread and Wine separately. But the Sacrament may be received in both kinds simultaneously, in a manner approved by the bishop.

When the celebrant is assisted by a deacon or another priest, it is customary for the celebrant to administer the consecrated Bread and the assistant the Chalice. When several deacons or priests are present, some may administer the Bread and others the Wine. In the absence of sufficient deacons and priests, lay persons licensed by the bishop according to the canon may administer the Chalice.

If the consecrated Bread or Wine does not suffice for the number of communicants, the celebrant is to return to the Holy Table, and consecrate more of either or both, by saying

Hear us, O heavenly Father, and with thy (your) Word and Holy Spirit bless and sanctify this bread (wine) that it, also, may be the Sacrament of the precious Body (Blood) of thy (your) Son Jesus Christ our Lord, who took bread (the cup) and said,"This is my Body (Blood)." *Amen.*

or else the celebrant may consecrate more of both kinds, saying again the words of the Eucharistic Prayer, beginning with the words which follow the Sanctus, and ending with the Invocation (in the case of Eucharistic Prayer C, ending with the narrative of the Institution).

When the services of a priest cannot be obtained, the bishop may, at discretion, authorize a deacon to distribute Holy Communion to the congregation from the reserved Sacrament in the following manner:

1. After the Liturgy of the Word (and the receiving of the people's offering), the deacon reverently places the consecrated Sacrament on the Altar, during which time a communion hymn may be sung.

2. The Lord's Prayer is then said, the deacon first saying,"Let us pray in the words our Savior Christ hath (has) taught us."

3. And then, omitting the breaking of the Bread, the deacon proceeds with what follows in the liturgy as far as the end of the postcommunion prayer, and then dismisses the people.

If any of the consecrated Bread or Wine remain, apart from any which may be required for the Communion of the sick, or of others who for weighty cause could not be present at the celebration, or for the administration of Communion by a deacon to a congregation when no priest is available, the celebrant or deacon, and other communicants, reverently eat and drink it, either after the Communion of the people or after the Dismissal.

A hymn may be sung before or after the postcommunion prayer.

## Disciplinary Rubrics

If the priest knows that a person who is living a notoriously evil life intends to come to Communion, the priest shall speak to that person privately, and tell *him* that *he* may not come to the Holy Table until *he* has given clear proof of repentance and amendment of life.

The priest shall follow the same procedure with those who have done wrong to their neighbors and are a scandal to the other members of the congregation, not allowing such persons to receive Communion until they have made restitution for the wrong they have done, or have at least promised to do so.

When the priest sees that there is hatred between members of the congregation, *he* shall speak privately to each of them, telling them that they may not receive Communion until they have forgiven each other. And if the person or persons on one side truly forgive the others and desire and promise to make up for their faults, but those on the other side refuse to forgive, the priest shall allow those who are penitent to come to Communion, but not those who are stubborn.

In all such cases, the priest is required to notify the bishop, within 14 days at the most, giving the reasons for refusing Communion.